A PLEA
FROM THE
ANGELS

Messages from St. Michael,
the Archangel

A PLEA
FROM THE
ANGELS

Messages from St. Michael,
the Archangel

Denise R. Cooney

AMETHYST BOOKS

First published in the United Kingdom in 1996 by
AMETHYST BOOKS
Lime Tree House, Swalcliffe,
Banbury, Oxfordshire OX15 5EH

Reprinted twice in 1996

Printed by The Guernsey Press

ISBN 0–944256–74–0

Amethyst Books are distributed in the USA by
NATIONAL BOOK NETWORK
4720 Boston Way, Lanham, MD 20706 (tel. 1800 462 6420)

and in the rest of the world by
GATEWAY BOOKS
The Hollies, Wellow, Bath BA2 8QJ (tel. 01225 835127)

DEDICATION

This book Is Lovingly Dedicated to My Friend and Fellow Student of Metaphysics and Spirituality, Nick Bamforth.

Many thanks to those who have contributed to the completion of this book: Jim Pluskota, Gay Thormann, Carleen Cole, Lynn Marasco, Marie Toohey, Susanne Winter, Lauren Thomas, Louise Gimbert, Julie Weiss, and to my family and friends for their support.

Table of Contents

INTRODUCTION

Many people have asked me where I get my information? What inspires me? Well, my information and inspiration come from many places. They come from life experience. They come divinely from Spirit.

Recently, I have had a series of losses. In the past few years I have witnessed the passing of my friend, Diane Tucker. I have lost my twin sons, Michael and Zachery, shortly after they were born. Falling on the heels of their death was the loss of my friend of many years, Tom Simpson. Most recently, I have lost my long time friend, student, publisher and past lifetime brother, Nick Bamforth.

Nick's passing has made a significant shift in my life. With every death comes a ripple in the pool of our consciousness that brings up other losses and changes in our lives. Healing is a process that many of us take for granted. If we feel sick we know we will get better. If we hurt we know the pain will heal.

Sometimes we wonder if these experiences will ever stop. I have wondered why the pain of losing someone to death is so very painful. Why does it take so long to heal? Most of us are students of spirituality and know that death is just an exit from physical life into the next stage. However, when we are personally affected by death, it takes on a new meaning. We realize that no matter how much we study spirituality there will be tears. There will be pain. There will be a time to grieve. How long do we grieve?

In the Western Culture we are given three days off from work to grieve and then it is back to business as usual. People we know are afraid to talk to us about how we feel. They are terrified to get into conversations about death. We treat death as if it is taboo. We can talk about sex, abortions and birth but not death.

I am telling you that it takes time to heal. One year and maybe longer. As a holiday or anniversary occurs you realize that you will never be able to share that moment again with that special someone here on the physical plane. Time does help heal.

We, as a group, sat one evening and Michael channeled a very special message about death and why the pain is so deep. I will attempt to cover as much of the session as I can remember.

"You wonder why the pain of losing a loved one is so deep. On the physical plane if someone is in an accident you can see their pain. You give them the time it takes to recover. If someone is in a body cast you would not expect that person to come to work. In fact, if a friend suggested otherwise you would be horrified at their lack of compassion."

"When a person sustains a loss of a loved one whether it be a child, mother, father, brother, sister, life partner or friend, most people do not offer the same compassionate feelings. For a week or two you can tolerate them being upset. However, if their upset state lasts longer than that, most of you wonder when they are going to get over it. When are they going to get on with their lives? It is because you cannot see their pain. Or you may not have gone through a similar experience. That may cause you to become hasty in your judgment of others."

"Let me explain the principles of Love. When someone falls in love with another there is a wonderful bonding of energy. Imagine, if you will, vines and tendrils intertwining together. That intertwining, that bonding with another goes into your body and meshes with your vessels, organs, nerve endings and brain."

"In other words, that person becomes part of you. When falling in love, I am sure all of you have experienced a bonding process that gives you a sensation of complete joy. During that time you literally change the way you eat and think. This is the process of becoming one. In a spiritual marriage (one that is not on a legal document) there is great joy. If for one reason or another the partnership changes, let's say one person in the relationship becomes frightened and wants out, then there is great pain for both partners. They are literally being ripped apart. You cannot see it on the physical plane but you experience it in the body."

"In regards to relationships, if it is a spiritual bond, they will usually get back together. Both parties will again experience bliss if they have completed their karma. But if one of the partners is still in love and the other is not then they will continue to experience the pain until they let go."

"In death there is a different process. The person of your desire is no longer on the physical plane. The pain is so intense when you lose a child. It is as if part of your body has been ripped apart. The pain is intense when you lose a parent or partner. Imagine these tendrils and vines intertwined with your veins, vessels, organs, bones and brains being severed. That is why it hurts so much. Literally you are walking around with your spiritual body ripped open. Imagine walking around with your nerve endings exposed on your body!"

"Have compassion for those in pain. Have compassion for yourself when grieving. Yes, the person you love has made transition and is now on a different plane of consciousness. Yes, you may believe in God and feel guilty for having this pain. Release your guilt. There is nothing to feel guilty about. Some of the guilt may be based on thinking that you should know better."

"You are human. You grieve. Knowing that someone is on another plane is more of a concept than a reality. For now you still want to see the person. You need to allow yourself some time to heal. You study the realm of spirit. Allow yourself to be human. Christ cried as Jesus the man when he knew he was going to die. Allow yourselves to look at the Master and know that he has set the example."

"Take time to be gentle with yourself. Cry, get angry, feel your emotions. When you stuff or bury your emotions then you will experience disease later on in your life. Your heart cannot hold up with that much of a burden. Remember the body reflects what your thoughts and feelings are. Go and be who you are inside, not what others think you need to be. So it is."

Michael has powerful insights when it comes to dealing with challenges in life. At this present moment I have a challenge that I know will turn out for the highest and best. I know that love is a powerful agent of change. I know that my life is going to change in a way I have never imaged.

The passing of Nick out of my physical life has given me the courage to make the changes that I must make in my life. I feel that I am going to move from where I am. Relationships have taken on a new meaning for me. I am in a situation that I have never experienced before. I know that it is a past lifetime of karmic connection. Because it is karmic I have been told by my guides to allow God to take charge and all will unfold. Nick's death has released for me a greater capacity to love and understand. From each ending we always experience a new beginning.

Now some of you have asked is this really Michael the Archangel? As I can best explain this, yes. A portion of Michael channels through me as well as through others.

There are many people on this earth who have become open "mouthpieces" for God. I am one of them. If you really knew me then you would know that it is truly God's choice. In "Beyond A Master" and "What On Earth Is Happening?" I explain what channeling is.

I have heard some say, "No one can channel Angels." I've heard others say it can happen. Either way I am just doing the work I am told to do.

Peace - Denise

A PLEA
FROM THE
ANGELS

Messages from St. Michael,
the Archangel

Lessons in Working on the Self

Michael: January 7, 1993

In the first place, I'd like to say "good evening" and I would like to make a few suggestions. It's quite funny! You will have to look at this situation of the individualized self by imagining yourselves as grapes. We have the grapes growing on the vine. Over here we have burgundy. Over there we have zinfandel. Over there we have your regular household green grapes and over there we have beautiful concord grapes. The thing that is funny is the concord grape is starting to think it's more intelligent than the cabernet sauvignon. The cabernet sauvignon seems to think well, "I'm a much finer refined wine, so therefore I'm a better grape than you so come and follow me." There is another grape saying, "No, no, no."

So what we have here is a very amusing situation where each and every one of you needs to see how you are interacting with each other. I'm finding a bunch of serious self-fulfilled, self-interested individuals, and the thing is: you need to become really aware of this.

When you continue to do your spiritual work the thing you have to focus in on is yourself and your only serious contact is between you and Divine Beingness. And that's it. All other things on the external path are of a lightened nature. It's not up to you to regulate, dictate, dominate or to predesignate how someone else's progress is going. It doesn't really matter. Be in alignment with one another. Be supportive of one another. And that's it! There's nothing else that we can do, unless you really feel Divine Consciousness flowing through you.

That centered beingness that says "I have wisdom to speak!" as opposed to saying, " I have wisdom, I am wise and I have spoken." This is what we are seeing. You need to let go of the rope, drop the little monk shroud, and you need to just be yourself. If you continue to stay self-centered you're going to find yourself caught up in some big old nasty darkside dragon going, " Yum, tasty little morsel for today." So the thing is, I, Michael, want you, if you can (and this is a big thing to ask) to just have fun.

The thing is, you have to understand your inner voice. The whole year is going to be about inner voice, inner voice, inner voice. INNER VOICE! !! Getting in touch and tapping into your own angels, energy and vibration. If you need to tap into me, tap into me. If you need to tap into any of the other angels they are available for you. It's really important that in the heralding in of the workers you work with the angels. The angels set pace.

We're the ones that set palms down before Christ enters the room. If you want to, tap into that. That's more important than tapping into conspiracies or tapping into tabloid effect energy or tapping into what we are going to be hearing. This is the year that we are going to be hearing about the aliens and everything else. This is the year for a lot of confusion, a lot of mental and emotional confusion.

It is imperative that you stay away from the news and do not get hooked on the news. If you need to know the weather, learn about the weather. But even better than learning the weather, try to read nature. Try to feel the changes within by observing signs. Maybe you'll have to hear the weather report first and then look to see what nature is telling you. But it's going to be very important to learn the signs. Start by looking and smelling the air and looking at the leaves or the way the birds are flying or the tilt in the grass. Be open to what is occurring around you or the way the energy and vibration is affecting you. It's going to be very important for you to understand weather. A lot of sudden weather changes, as I told you, would happen and there are some more yet to come. It's important that you start working and developing your aspect of being able to be in touch with nature. It's even more important this year (and the years to come).

You're going to have to really work on a lot of protective devices this year in keeping out the astral entities that are presenting themselves as aliens and certain thought forms. There will be monster like energies reeking havoc on the planet and occasionally they will take physical being size and you will think that they are robots but they are really energy vibrations that are being sent here from mind mass hallucination. So the thing is, you're going to really have to work with yourself this time.

If you can, avoid certain energy centers. If you can, avoid New York City, avoid it, incredible, just cut it out of your life. If you can, avoid New York. Go in only for specific things that you have to do, avoid that energy. It's an energy vortex that's going in a counter clockwise direction and all energies around it are going clockwise. It's going to try and envelope into this tornado-like energy and try to wild out into these outlying regions. It's important that you be collected within yourself. You have to learn to be able to insulate yourself from the vibrations that are there.

You'll have the normal stuff such as minor irritations at home, at work, with friends, and the everyday things. Life can be the commercial that takes you away from the main movie which is God! You need to be able to focus your attention on the Divine. The mundane can be so intoxicating that the illusion takes you away from your spiritual nature.

The thing that you really need to develop is a more direct line with yourselves. Continue to do ceremony, but please understand the power of ceremony. Understand that not everyone can do ceremony. Please understand that there is a difference between ritual and ceremony. If you're doing a ritual, do not call it a ceremony because if you don't know what you're doing you're going to evoke higher powers and that is dangerous. A ritual or a prayer is a sacred thing to do. In a ceremony, you are commanding major spirit, folks. So if you don't know what you're doing, do not do ceremony. Do rituals instead.

Ritual is a little higher up on a vibrational level than a prayer but a ritual is something that is harmless. It's equalized energy. It's something even a child can do without supervision, but when you go into ceremony, calling in the big guns, you don't know what kind of karma backlash you're going to have on yourself. It's the last thing you want to do. So these are things to remember whenever you enter into prayer, into ceremony, into ritual. It's a highly evolved state of consciousness, it is not a joke, not anything to be taken lightly, it's a very powerful aspect of Divine Beingness.

Now some of you may be curious as to what is happening on an energy and vibrational level right now. The Masters, the angels, Mary, all of the male and female masters are joining together. They are working hand in hand doing a lot of work at this moment in time. They are working in the physical plane by bringing in a lot of ripples of energy and vibration of power. You know that when you push something into water there are a lot of waves. If you go into a large body of water and you throw in a big boulder there is a big splash and it blinds everybody temporarily. That's what's going to happen with this backlash of spiritual energy. Temporarily there will be a backlash. The earth changes such as: the flooding, the tornadoes and all of the things that are happening are part of the cleansing process. It is causing a tremendous amount of chaos on the Earth right now.

There will be more civil wars and more wars in the Middle East and that's a playing out of the darkside in order to fulfill the Book of Revelations. The Armageddon state of consciousness is trying to keep from individuals their belief or their sensitivity in Divine Beingness, their Divine prayer, the Divine self. So you have to understand that there is going to be a continuation and ripping apart of the Bible, of ridiculing and belittling people who are in the religious orders, more assaults on them, more of an outpouring of a disregard to spirituality, and spitting in the face of God. You are going to see more and more of this kind of human action happening. It's revealing in the animalistic nature of humanity.

There are many new energy vibrations. Things are coming into the planet. This is why you need to detach from the news because this kind of constant bombardment of "what's happening" is coming from the darkside. There are going to be casualties. People are going to be taken down. It's just the way it is. So there is going to be some physical carnage of individuals doing spiritual work. It's just the way it is. Not that they haven't protected themselves. This is war. And in this vibration, and in this final settling up - it's like this big karmic debt finally being paid up.

Someone doesn't want to pay the debt. Someone doesn't want to give it up, or say okay. Then they literally have to be evicted out of this energy field. So in the end, after all this turmoil and all the prophecies are fulfilled, Divine Beingness will establish Divine Balance. Divine Balance will occur everywhere but in a shape and form that this Earth is now. The Earth may not be the shape and form we see it in right now because it does have to enter into a higher octave.

If you plug into the news you're going to start being taken down and will say, "I see the good happening but there's so much bad happening. As far as I can physically see and physically hear I'm getting hooked into things that are making me forget to pray and to love fellow beings. I'm hearing things that are making me hate." And so, if you hate or learn to dislike the same people who are putting out hatred, you're on the same level. They're winning the war. So the thing is, that to neutralize their campaign, <u>again</u> try and see the God and Christ in all people.

This is going to be an intense year of refocusing. Every single person in this room is going to get off their center at some point. You'll be in fear or confusion saying, "Can't you really see what's happening? Oh my God, can't you see what's happening?" When you see that person losing it, you're going to have to surround that person in a lot of light.

19

It's going to be a very difficult and powerful time for allowing yourself not to go limp, not to be blank, or be indifferent or apathetic towards others. Say, "Okay, there's nothing I can do about that situation." or, "This is what I can do about the situations in my life and this is what I can do to help create change."

This is the year that you have to really think about activating in yourself whatever work you want to do to create a change. You have no choice after this year. You have to think about what you do to create change in this world. Whether it's as simple as just being a good person, donating time to a charity or sharing vegetables with your neighbor. This is the year you not only open your mouth, but this is the year you do as your mouth says.

If you do not do what you believe in your heart of hearts what you need to do, the tasks in the next following years will be that much harder for you. This is your window in time to do it, to find that oasis, that respite. That this is still while I am alive, this is still my dream, my goal, this is still what I do. Amidst all this chaos, I am still capable of finding humanity in myself and this is what I do.

The moment it becomes a burden, you stop. You no longer do it. Then find something else to do. If it's a burden you're no longer doing it from the heart. If it becomes all encompassing and you don't know how to do it, you have so much fear, and so on. Stop! Give it up. Don't do it! Do what you know needs to be done. This may be the year when you change six, seven, eight or nine different things and you've already done three, four and five different things, but you do what you do because you know it needs to be done. You don't do it because you have to do it. If you're not doing it from the flow of spirit then you're not doing it. And then you can't complain about it to anyone else. If it's your personality self, then ask yourself, "Am I doing this because I like to, or because it sounds good when I tell other people?" So this is really a year of reflection. The mirror is going to be held up to you very closely. But the mirror is also going to be held up to everyone else this year, very closely.

What I'm trying to do is give you a hint of how to get through this mirroring effect, because you're going to see a lot of people losing it this year. A lot of mental breakdowns. A lot of wars. A lot of things, because, people can't face up to themselves. So what they're going to do is reek havoc on someone else. This is the year you stay away. You do what you do. You hang out with your family. You do the best that you can do. If your family isn't satisfactory, if they're not supportive, you stay away from your family. That's it. Think God. Divine Beingness. Divine Spiritual Family. This is what I have. I have the Angels. I have Christ. I have God who created me. God allowed me to be born into a family situation, but this is not my spiritual family. This is the family that gives me my lessons. So the thing is, you need to on some level, hook up esoterically with that spiritual family and realize it really is the Mother/Father/Divine Creator. You are a child and therefore, everyone around you is your brother and sister. And on that level, then you connect with the brothers and sisters around you.

But do not play games with one another! Do not throw out your anger, become secretive, petty or gossipy. Gossiping is NOT allowed! Very, very inappropriate! It only brings down situations, people and conditions around you. You might as well go out there and be doing something incredibly vile, because that's one of the most vile things you can do to one another. So this is something you really have

21

to think about: Is this constructive? Destructive? Is this gossip? So it's going to be a really powerful year. And anything you say, think or do is going to really boomerang back to you at an incredibly powerful rate.

So that's all I have to say, good-bye and have a good evening. Through Divine Light, Divine Love and Divine Wisdom. I know you're going to make it through this year, and it's going to be fun. I have a lot more to say, but another time, and so it is...

Levels of Consciousness

Michael: Feb. 11, 1993

Basically, life is about sitting and waiting and allowing the Dynamics of Truth to come through. You see that happen with the energies and vibrations that are happening right now The intensity of energy that comes in from various planes of consciousness creates an upliftment, a transformation or transmutation into this plane of consciousness. This plane of consciousness, as you know it, no longer exists. The physical plane and the properties of the physical plane have been altered so what you knew life to be is changing. If everyone is saying, "Gee, this isn't the life I remember." This is true! We are now entering another plane of consciousness. The transition into a new plane of consciousness is not easy for anyone.

What is happening is that we are now entering into a lower plane of consciousness. Right now! This is why there are so many volatile, violent, hostile energies happening. You are now entering into the psyche of the human consciousness. What you're really entering into is all of the stored energy of the entire historical creation of human beings since the beginning of time. It's an energy and vibration that is based on antiquity, the truth, human emotion, the inner workings and subconscious aspect of human kind. What you are entering is not the twilight zone, but entering into the human psyche. People are having a hard time dealing with what they've created. People are making up and creating falsified situations from racial problems, etc.

There are no racial problems, quite frankly. If you look at it from the standpoint of beingness, the problems are created within the minds of each and every individual. There are no racial problems. If you look at the problems of poverty. There is no real reason for poverty on your planet. It is created within the minds of each individual. Since on this planet, at this very moment, there is enough for each and every individual. It is the mind set of each and every individual; how they harbor, how they dole out, sustain and create, keep down and how they work as human beings. There is no reason on this planet why we need to worry about having cures for diseases. Many of the processes of disease (outside of the self-inflicted man-made diseases) will always exist as long as there is humanity because that is nature's way of creating a cleansing. For certain diseases there are no cures. Period!

The reason there is disease is because mankind's framework is such that it gives a lot of religious significance to having disease. The reason there are racial problems is mankind gives a lot of religious significance in having racial differences. The reason there is prosperity and poverty is that mankind has a lot of religious influence in creating this.

When I'm talking about religion I'm talking about dogma, creed and empty ritual. When I'm talking about spirituality, I'm talking about the teachers who came and are coming and are still coming and are here. They spread the word of the Dynamic laws of Truth. The religions that men follow are made up by man-made rules and belief systems in order to keep situations and people separated, creating boundaries and visions.

So the human dilemma that you're in right now, the human psyche that you're walking into right now is actually devoid of the consciousness of God. And at the same time, since humanity is created by Divine Consciousness and Divine Beingness, the darkside must reign before the light moves in to destroy the darkness. So what you can actually see here is the darkside that you are battling. The evil, is basically, the primordial aspect of humankind. The devil-like energy is the human beingness, the darkside, the side that does not know God. It is the side that knows man as power.

The reason I have asked all of you not to watch the news is because man's power is becoming incredibly strong. Focus in on God. Focus in on Spirit. Focus in on Truth. Allow yourselves to be who you truly are. It is going to be a time of revelation for yourselves so you can see where you are on your path. There are things about yourself that you are just going to have to accept. Your humanness needs to be accepted.

You have to accept your darkside before you move towards your light side. There is absolutely, on this planet, no reason for pollution. It is in the consciousness of man to create this. It is part of their religious structure. It is part of man's darkness to create a situation that the darkness must be destroyed. It is part of the religious structure in the human beingness.

You need to understand because mankind is so finite and refuses to accept the infinite, that it creates destruction as a way to be brought to its knees to cry, " I don't want to die." But in the death of the human beingness comes the birth of the Christ Consciousness. But the human beingness and its destruction of the human beingness sometimes loses sight of what the destruction actually means. It means the surrender, the loss of attachment, the letting go of.

If you find yourselves getting wrapped up in this world of illusion, do not read the paper, watch the news, listen to the radio, but rather read and focus in on those things of God right now. The world and the news will carry on without you. The world and the news do not need you to exist. They exist without you. They are part of the finite world of illusion and will continue to exist. If more people did not listen to the news, read the papers and focus in on the radio, people would then have to focus in on themselves. Racial problems and many other problems would come to a cessation, for there would be no energy feeding into them.

All of human kind right now is crying out "I am different." "I am selected." "You must take care of my individualistic needs." The dynamics of spirit is the encompassment of all into the ocean of consciousness, which God's presence resides in. Each droplet looses itself within the I AM to become one with God. In the sea of humanity each droplet wants to retain its own individuality. No longer do we have an ocean, we have raindrops that dissipate and disappear and lose themselves in the desert to evaporate and die.

When working on individualistic concepts, thinking that you're working on the whole to create a better Earth, think clearly. Is it because you wish to inflict your view on someone else? Or truly are you charged from Spirit saying, "I too hear the clarion call and am moving towards creating a higher realm."

I think this evening, in this short time, I have spoken of things that are even too hard for some of you to comprehend. Relax, re-listen and re-learn. If I ask you to do something it is not to be taken as a flip remark, but please think carefully upon these words this evening. And so it is.

Living Your Truth

Michael: February 18, 1993

Tonight, what I want to say is: When you really feel your inner strength; your inner beingness; the dynamics of the truth; knowledge, joy and wisdom, you are feeling who you really are. Why do you prevent yourself from projecting this image on you daily life? Why do you allow yourselves to play the roles that others expect you to play? Why do you slip out of who you are to please other people? Why aren't you allowing yourself to be who you really are? Why do you short change your knowledge? Why do you short change your joy, your humor, and all of the different aspects of yourselves?

You need to really focus in on the fact that if you enjoy the solidness that you feel when you come to these classes, then you must allow yourselves to feel the solidness of yourself twenty-four hours a day. This is not something you just do in church or meditation or with a group of like-minded people. This is the time for you to be who you are. This is this time for you to be that no-nonsense self. That truth filled, benevolent self. That compassionate self. That self who you know yourself to be. In your meditation this evening, each and everyone of you were willing to wear the robe of truth. To see yourselves in blues, golds, whites and other colors. You were allowing yourselves to see the radiance and beauty that you are.

But tomorrow morning when you go to work, you will not see that. You will see what other people project upon you. You will shortchange yourself. You will sit down and say the human test is too hard. I'm a failure at this, that and the other thing. You allow the creation of what others think of you to become you. What you've allowed yourself to be molded into will be how you present yourself that day. You will feel the heaviness of the Earth plane move through you. You may wonder what that heaviness is. It's the energy and vibration of humanity. The energies you felt tonight in prayer and meditation are the energies that you need to strive for on a daily basis.

You are sensitive. You need to understand that. You want to know why people are sick It is because they are not sensitive They have so many blocks. They are so rigid. They are in denial or in pain. They won't allow the God-life to flow through them. Therefore, they create illness.

Why are you sleepy and tired? There is less oxygen in the air. The energy is changing. There is tremendous pollution. But it is also due to the heaviness of the planets.

I'm not saying to study astrology. But the planets do influence the bodies. I said a long time ago that the Earth is moving into the heart chakra, the Sun being the head, the other planets being the representation of the chakras. Think about it? Twelve planets, nine that you see, ten with the sun, two yet undiscovered (Vulcan and the planet beyond). You as beings need to understand that the physicality of this Earth, the physicality of this plane of beingness is changing, Permanently. Forever. Thank goodness! And if it becomes a meteorite. Be it.

You can be in that state of beingness with or without a body. The Channel asks if you can go there first. No. You can go there last. But you can keep it as a memory, a place that you can enter occasionally and when you're ready, that's where you will live. You will be doing the work of the teachers, praising God twenty-four hours a day, chanting, praying, sending out the energies to help raise the consciousness of planets that are in a vibration lower than yourselves. That's what the Masters do, day in and day out. They pray for the lower consciousness to raise.

Masters have infinite patience, infinite perseverance. Because of their knowingness, they know that all beings created by Divine Beingness will return to where they came from. You as individuals are finite and cannot conceive that. Otherwise, you would not speak so cruelly, coldly and curtly of your fellow human beings. Your leaders do the best they can. Did I not tell you to pray for them and not to curse them. You curse them and by the power of your own words, those of you who say you're so in alignment with God, your curse weighs heavier than those on the street whose folly is a daily basis and their words wage not the same war as yours. Remember what side of the party line you're on. You are on the party line for creating a greater world for all humanity.

If you choose to be, like the pack, like everyone else, then you don't have to worry about your spiritual studies, or your spiritual truth. You can just blindly and glibly go along, skipping down Earth's little path. Taking this lifetime to waste your time being concerned about other people's business, criticizing them, berating them, judging them. It shows your own ignorance. This is why there's no time for gossip. You are not judge and jury.

There will be plenty of time for gossip about you when you make your transition and you look at your own Akashic records. When we pull forth the people you have hurt. Those you have spoken about.

29

Laughed about. Torn up. You judged them. See how they feel when they hear what you've said about them, especially friends. Now is the time to heal, release, forgive and let go, because you still have a body to do it in. When you don't, it will be the summation, the totality of the actions, deeds and words of your life. Think about that next time you open your big mouth to say something cruel about someone I'll be with you and I'll let you hear what you're saying and I'll let the person hear what you're saying. You'll see their tears. You'll see their pain. You'll see what you're doing that's so funny.

Meditate, enjoy your life, and pray and pray and pray. And so it is.

Working Towards a
Higher Level of Beingness

Michael: February 25, 1993

The first thing that I want to talk to you about this evening is how to work through your ego. How to transcend that energy. What you have invested in that ego. And how to move through that ego vibration so that you can really pull in the higher God vibration --the higher levels of enlightenment.

That's really what you're trying to do. You are trying to allow yourself to stay at a higher plane of beingness. You are trying to move through the ego and trying to go into that higher plane of beingness. As you move through the higher planes of beingness, you will finally reach that point of transition where you have gone beyond all the planes and you become God-Realized.

Why it is so difficult to make that transition is because there are so many identifications with the self and with the physical plane. People make personal identifications such as: what they're going to wear; how they're going to comb their hair; what kind of make-up they're going to put on; how they're going to shave or not shave and so on. It is the identification of the body, of the self, of the physical plane and its comings and goings on.

Now it's very difficult to move through this plane of consciousness and work toward higher beingness because you do get stuck here. This is a very fascinating place because no matter how many answers you get, you can think of more questions because the Divine Beingness, so to speak, has so many aspects of itself here on the physical plane. Some of these aspects are: people, life forms, trees, rocks, plants, animals, insects. All the different aspects. You can never ask enough questions because you'll never get enough answers due to so many countless beings here on the planet Earth.

So you, as an individualized self, encapsulated into your personality, need to do a lot of work in staying focused in on God. You are outside of yourself when you are not focused in on God. It is being focused in on the God presence that resonates and exists and embodies your being thus creating the soul consciousness in order to have life. And also working towards radiating to the center most part of your being and understanding that if you were to make transition today, tomorrow, next week, or the year after, however you die in this physical form -- its just one ending of the aspect of self.

Now how you die in the metaphysical or spiritual sense is the death of the self. It's no longer identifying yourself with the physical body. Now we're not talking about no longer taking a bath, changing your clothes or brushing your teeth. We're not talking about those kinds of things. However, there are some people who are in such a higher state of beingness or are so God-intoxicated that they cannot see this physical plane and do lose consciousness that they have a physical body and allow the physical body not to be taken care of. These are some of the people you see in institutions and some of the homeless you see in the street. They're very God intoxicated. They're not focused in on this Earth plane at all. They see God at all times. So the seeing of God and the feeling of that God presence to the outside world makes them appear to be crazy.

Then there are those individuals who can see God and work with God and be with and communicate with God and still maintain the physical body and maintain the physical plane, but they are not of this world. They are not wrapped up in the inner trappings. Many of these beings, if they are in a marriage state, are usually individuals who are much older. And at that point many of their children are raised and they are no longer in the traditional marriage situation but rather they're in a situation where their partner is their anchor whether their partner is male or female.

So when an individual is so absorbed in the state of beingness of God and you look into their eyes, you see the endless universe there. These are the same people who, when they touch you, can raise and lift your consciousness so that you are able to go into the higher planes that you have not made the transition to. What we're talking about is that final ascent out of all the inner workings and being immersed in the God State of Beingness. At that point, you can make the decision whether you want to come back. If you do come back, you come back as a Master. You come back heralding in and bringing in the God-man or God-woman to create balance on this planet.

You see, in the physical plane with the identification of all the small things that happen, and as you've all been talking, you need Consciousness to awaken you. You need Consciousness to shift you. Some of you come here already awake and we're not just talking about those in this room. We're talking about the overall Earth plane. Some people come in awake. They are born in the physical body very prepared to do the spiritual work. It's not unlike the children who come in who have acquired knowledge and they become the next Dalai Lama.

There are some people who come in and they are not aware until they are seven or eight years of age. Then they become aware of their spiritual status but forget because of the Earth plane consciousness that's around them only to be shaken up at a later point in their life. Sometimes it's through some severe situation, whether its a death or an accident or world wide catastrophic event. Then there are other individuals who just plod along the Earth and things come and happen and they have lesson upon lesson but they refuse to awaken.

So you have all asked questions and all had different answers towards what's the difference between the creation. In Divine Beingness, God created all things. In Divine Beingness, you as actors and actresses in this plane of consciousness for God and in order to know yourself for God to come back to yourself, to understand yourself as God, you must go through a series of acts, as you have in a play.

From Divine Beingness, from the point of inception of yourself into the plant state, there is a predetermined amount of lives that you will move through, predetermined amount of lives that you will experience and it's up to you whether you move on the path or not.

There comes a time in each and every individual's awareness that an inner alarm clock goes off and says, "Gee, I've incarnated over 30,000 times and I still haven't gotten it. Maybe I need a bigger lesson because every time I'm in this place called the Akashic Records and every time I'm in this place called the Earth plane, and every time I go through this and I see that I make the same mistakes over again, I call in all of the lessons, most intensely to myself to create a new being, to raise my level of consciousness. So what will I create for myself? I need to create a series of situations that without a doubt makes me recognize that my personal life is not as important as the quality of my life."

Individuals create for themselves situations where they can at any given moment decide to undertake the task of "quality of life". And at any given moment, that individual, whether he, she, child, adult, male or female comes into a situation, especially a family situation, any time you have a death you have a raising of consciousness for the entire family. So what you're doing, within the small group mind, is creating situations to create growth. So as one person grows, another person may shut down. Another person may go into denial. But, there is always one who grows. Whether they grow aware of their anger, their frustration, or whatever emotion, an individual truly does grow.

And the individuals who are making transition and are yearning for God-realization feel it more powerfully than the yearning for individualized consciousness. It is that innermost aspect of wanting to know oneself as God. Your innermost consciousness wants to express itself as God. You will go through any lengths to allow yourself to awaken yourself to your potential. And many people awaken themselves to their potential through suffering and death.

So the creation of the death state, the creation of disease and of allowing this to happen to yourself, as an individualized personal self, is the most noble thing you can do for yourself. You sacrifice the ego in order for the self to know God in the most sacrificial way that you could. You knew internally that your ego was so thick that you needed a bombshell or dynamite to blast through. You needed to get through some level of fear that was so overwhelming. And then there are people who make transition that are extremely at peace. Most people die in peace. The creation and the death state are one in the same. There is no shift. There is no difference, there is no either/or within the dichotomy or the dichotomies of the dichotomies. The reality tries to speak through. The reality says, "I need to know myself as God."

In the human plane because your consciousness is finite the infinite is hard to grasp. Remember, you have finite human consciousness. Finite consciousness sees pain and suffering as not the most desired accessory. I'm sure if all of you had the option to shop in a really fine store and you had the cash or you had the option to have a piece of cement attached to your feet and thrown in the ocean, I'm sure you would rather take the cash and spend it in the store than go to the bottom of the ocean. But in essence, your inner consciousness wants to go to the innermost ocean of Divine Beingness and Love. It is the trappings of the physical plane that makes you think the most desired outcome is for the total beauty and bounty and beauty is how you perceive it. Joy is how you perceive it. Health is how you perceive it. Do not tell a parent whose child is deformed that they have an ugly child, or a parent who is seeing their child die, that that child is hopeless, or a husband that he might as well let go of his wife, and do not tell yourself when you see a beggar in the street that you must turn away.

When you can raise your consciousness to the eye of God and see the beauty in every single fashion, every single motion and every single wave, when you can understand that the violence of mankind is an outpouring, a crying out to the heavens for help because the direction of love is lost. When you see one man slaying the other in anger and violence and senseless killing, you can see that the love light within the human being has been turned low, low, low. You can see that at this planet's inception when love was the outpouring, when love was the dynamic that created this planet, the human being was given their own free will to make their own way back to God. The free will itself and the condition that humanity is in today has created a separation that might as well be the separation of the Grand Canyon between man, humankind and the God Consciousness itself.

But since in Spirit there is no time and there is no space, in the twinkling of an eye, if you as individualized beings could stop asking individualized questions and try to see yourselves more as a holistic entity, a holistic beingness then you will understand what that phrase means, "And this too I shall bless as good and this too I shall bless as love and this too I see through the eyes of God." If you can allow yourselves a moment of empowerment to believe this, accept, absorb and embrace this, not when you're feeling the most peace filled but when you're feeling the most turmoil.

The darkside likes to shift within you in, each and every person and condition. When you turn on the television, and this is why I'm saying don't watch television right now. When you turn on the television you get sucked into the violence, the anger, frustration, racial problems, the sexual gender-based, disease-based, everything based situations that are happening on the Earth. If you can, with fortitude, look and see that these are children of Earth. These are beings who are now orphaned. Sorely missing their parents. Trying to find love through someone else. Trying to establish a power base within a blank or empty power base. Trying to substitute a government for a parent, a missile or guns for love and affection. If you could see it through the eyes of God, if you could see the people dying, as the beings who are here to create an awakening of compassion. If you could see the people being born as beings who did not make it in the last lifetime to raise to a level of higher consciousness. These are beings who are rushing here after a previous incarnation to learn a lesson. If you can have compassion for the new beings coming here. If you can generate love and keep your veil of deception away from your eyes, you will find more truth circulating from within the center most part of yourself then you've ever know before. Now is the time for raising up of consciousness.

You may not be able personally or to single handed release yourself of the duties of your ego. You may not, single handed be able to release yourself from your confusion. But what you can do is you can start to empower and enable yourself to be able to make baby steps toward trying to see the dynamics of the oneness and blessing situations and seeing the good.

This is the hard part, for when our parents act up, when our relationships act up, when our employees and employers act up, when other humans around us act up, it's very difficult to maintain that peace. See, as you are an individualized drop in the consciousness of God, you are also an individualized drop in the human consciousness. And it's very difficult to go deep and inward when you are on the surface of the human consciousness and the wave is going with great movement. How difficult it is for that one single little droplet to try and remain individualized and at the bottom of the ocean. You get caught up in the swell. So as beings of truth and God, maybe as an assignment for one day, is to just say to yourself "and this too is good."

I give thanks and so it is.

The Inner Sanctuary and The Sun, Food & Water

Michael: April 1, 1993

In the Book of Revelations it is written that there will be darkness for three days and light for three days. If you, as individuals, understand the true metaphysical meaning behind this, then you know that the Earth is starting to enter into the darkness. And this is what the darkness feels like. This is what the darkness of the sun feels like.

We're talking about the analogies that are in your Bible. We're talking about the analogies that are in all your metaphysical books that have been here since the beginning of time. People are looking for physical signs of earth changes and earth consciousness. Does not today and the last few days feel like a darkening of the sun within yourselves?

In order for you to get through the purification process, you have to be able to always return to the inner sanctuary of your higher consciousness. It is not the physical manifestation of being without sun. It is the psychological, emotional, psychic, spiritual feeling of being without sun. You must allow yourself at every turn, every moment, every juncture, every footstep to understand that each person you speak to, each person that speaks to you, is the voice of God. Each word that comes out of your mouth is the voice of God. And you constantly have options, moment by moment, to speak in the light or to speak in the darkness, to speak the truth or to speak falsehood, depending on how it affects you.

Also, it depends on how focused you are in your own highest of the high and how you are focused on their highest of the high in order to be able to penetrate through the facade of the personality self. The personality self who is crying out for help like a drowning victim. Or the personality self who is swimming, relaxed and poised and focused in on Spirit regardless of the situation they might be in.

So when you run into individuals who are causing you to have emotional shifts and changes in your own energy sphere, your own life sphere. You must ask yourself; "How am I listening?" You must ask yourself, "What view am I taking? Am I taking an aggressive stance that is automatically making someone else take an aggressive stance?" Or "If aggression is coming at me and it is not what I'm putting out to this person, I need to look at this individual from a different angle and understand that the personality, the temperament, the words, the lack that is within them is being portrayed in the personality that they are trying to project at me."

What you are seeing over and over and over again are damaged beings. You yourself are a damaged being What is happening is that you are trying to the best of your capabilities to do rehabilitation. But when other damaged beings come at you, you recognize the damage within them because it's the same damage you have within yourself. You just refuse to see that it's the same damage you have within yourself. It's distasteful to look at it because you think you've overcome it. It can be trying. It can be exasperating. It can be infuriating and frustrating.

So the thing is, as hard as it sounds to do, you need to try to the best of your capability to pull back. You need to go find that time, find that inner sanctuary. You have to have that inner sanctuary twenty, thirty, forty, fifty or sixty minutes a day to talk to yourself, Divine Consciousness and God. You say, "I can't see the different angle that you've asked me to look for. I have my faith cranked up on high but the energies around me are very strong, pulling me down." Shift gears, be good to yourself, go out and laugh. Release and let go, shake your arms. Most of you forget to release the energy back down to the Earth after meditation. You just open your eyes. Really shake that energy back down to the ground. Shake it out, otherwise you store it up and store it up. When it's finished, it's over, let it go, let it go and fertilize the consciousness around you. It is going to be heavier. I did not say it's going to be lighter. But you're experiencing some of the heaviness.

And remember, I said to you many months ago, if you're tired, lay down. If you feel that you're falling asleep, then you need to. You are stepping into a battle that you may not be strong enough to handle on your own. Instead of eating through lunch go to sleep. Instead of having chitter chatter with your fellow employees, go take a nap. And if you can't fall asleep, allow yourself to see your energy being changed, transformed, released. Go back and be rejuvenated. Bring a tape with you, bring some music that makes you relax and you enjoy and be peace filled. Try whatever you can to create balance and center.

Your spring will be short, your summer will be impactful and the food supply has shifted. Forget all these different aspects that are happening at the same time. You're going to have record crops probably in tomatoes and zucchini and record lows in certain fruits and things that you usually enjoy. With the amount of rain that has come up, the chemicals and the pesticides have been driven down further into the water wells and water tables and at the same time the residues are coming up higher and being ingested by the dairy animals. If you can, try to be a vegetarian, now would be the time. If you can, try and stay away from dairy products, now would be the time. If you can, try to eat organic as much as possible. Even though the organic foods will be contaminated by pesticides, not because they are being sprayed but because the pesticide residue is coming up from the soil, it is worth the extra dollars that you spend for yourself and your family. They will help to prevent the amount of kidney, eye and bronchial problems that will start happening to people and children that have never had problems before. You're going to see series of rashes and skin aliments like you have never seen before. It is not all atmospheric. It is going to be in the food. It is up to you whether you choose to do these thing or not.

I cannot say too much any longer about the sun. Protect your skin again this summer. This summer's heat is going to start being so high. You're going to start noticing your car fading faster than usual in the sun if you do not keep it in the garage. You will notice your plastic seats splitting. So with the heat of the sun and the plastics within your car, just think of the fumes you're going to be breathing as soon as you get in your car. Leave the doors open with the windows down. Check your air conditioning supply because you could be poisoning your own selves in your own vehicles while staying cool. It's a slow and insidious process.

Now it's not all bad. That's some of the worse that will be happening. The food chain is what you need to eat to sustain you and keep you alive. I decided that would be hard enough to hear. It's going to be costly. You're going to find it being almost the same buying organic as what you would be buying in the store. So seek out now the places to go and, if you can, try and buy organic coffee. It's a big shift, do it little by little, but have it done by the end of May, the beginning of June. Very slowly, change over your household. See if you can get your water purified if you still use tap water.

There are going to be many big earth and energy changes taking place. With the advent of all these changes is also the advent of much spiritual awakening and spiritual insight. So you will understand that when you speak to others you will be hearing God. When you really listen, you will hear the Christ voice speaking through the person that you are talking to and you will wake up with revelation and look at them as if they are a highly blessed being. And when you speak to them they will not know what you are talking about because they were just saying what they were thinking or they were just saying what they believe.

Another thing, telepathy right now is so strong that I'm sure almost all of you at work have experienced someone saying to you, "I was just thinking about that." or "I was just going to change that station." Understand, you're becoming highly sensitive now and because you're highly sensitive, people's emotions and vibrations are going to affect you even more. It doesn't matter what colors, what candles, what crystals, what thistles, what tassels you use. It's meditating! It's grounding! It's staying focused! It's being in the water! That works. Swim, shower, do something! Be in the water. It is very important!

So, what do you want to know?

Q. What would be everyday spirituality that we don't see as spiritual?

A. Waking up is spiritual, so is getting out of bed, taking off your pajamas, going to the bathroom, making your bed, cleaning your floor, having food, getting in your car, getting gas, driving, looking at people around you. It's all spirit. Do you need any more examples?

A. No.

Q. How is our air-conditioning dangerous?

A. What I'm talking about, with the heat the way it is and with the sun's rays not filtering the way they've been, you're seeing a different type of release of gasses than you've ever seen before. This is why you're going to see the quicker deterioration of your car interiors. The fabric in your car may become brittle. If you have these fumes and haven't properly ventilated your car and you have on your air conditioner and it hasn't been properly checked with the freon, it's going to yet create, not a formaldehyde or arsenic, but those type of gasses that can create a lethargic feeling. Filters are really very important to filter out particulate matter and microbes.

Q. Filters for water, boiling tap water, bathing, is this dangerous?

A. Boiling water creates more toxins, so you are actually releasing carcinogens every time you boil water. Bathing isn't quite as bad, unless your body is a big wound. You're not bringing a lot of toxins into your body. Radon is released in the water, when you take a shower, as a gas. Almost everyone's house right now has high levels of radon. See, with the Earth shifting, the center core is pushing up a lot of different materials and you're going to find that gasses are building. Radon is a definite problem in this entire area, meaning New Jersey and Pennsylvania. A much bigger problem in New York State. They don't really understand the long-term effects. Radon combined with the

44

electromagnetic field actually helps the electromagnetic fields that would normally stop at a certain wave length. The radon actually enhancing the field. So if you have a small field, the radon makes it bigger. With the electromagnetic field causing destruction in the radon gasses, the radon itself gets highly excited and the diffusement and disbursement changes a little. So where the gas might be easily released by opening a window with proper ventilation, it looks like it's making it a little bit heavier. Therefore, you need real circulation moving through. There are many different things happening that science may or may not come up with, but you'll probably be reading about it soon. Please don't forget to take Vitamin E and A because some of you are experiencing eye problems and are not putting 2 + 2 together. I've been telling you to wear your sunglasses and you do it for a while and then stop. I'm very concerned about your eyes, so please make sure your children, your family, wears glasses.

Q. How can we better use telepathy to communicate with people?

A. Well, you can practice with people now say, at 8:00 p.m. on Thursday. I want to set up a conversation with you and then confer back the following day, not that night, and see what you picked up on or did you or did you forget, and that type of thing.

Q. Aggression coming from people, especially my father.

A. If you can understand that an individual is multi-faceted and the aggression you're feeling and picking up from your father is that there's some issues going on with him and when that energy comes at you, it pushes old buttons. It's very easy to fall into not feeling good about yourself or wanting him to shut up or whatever it is you've been thinking. You need to allow yourself to pull back and say, "Okay, my father is hurting, there is obviously a sign that he is hurting, it bothers me that I have to see that he's hurting. What I need to do is make an observation for myself that, "Boy, am I really getting pulled into this." And when you can make that observation, at the moment of his aggression, hold onto that memory, "I really got pulled into this, this really bothers me, let me see what this is all about. Is it about being a victim?"

Then you ask yourself a series of questions. Then what you can do when you identify that you're starting to pull back is to really allow yourself to see your father healed by love. Allow yourself to see yourself being healed by love, not so he changes, not so the aggression dissipates and goes away, but so you as an individual are focused in on the love between you as opposed to the aggression that's coming at you.

Do you understand? You're not trying to change the situation. You're trying to reach into a higher aspect of the situation. The depth of the situation is that there's a lack of love at that moment in time. That's the real depth of the situation. You cannot see that love at that moment in time. So when that situation comes up, you really need to pull the love in and almost pull back like an outside observer and go "that's really interesting, this is how I respond to that kind of a feeling and I always respond this way. Let me pull back and make an observation." That's the best way I can describe to you what you can do for yourself.

I will end for this evening and so it is.

Lessons for Easter

Michael: April 1993

This evening, as you open up into the higher time, allow yourself to know what the "Christ return" means --as the Christ left his physical body, as the Christ ascended into the higher planes of consciousness. You as individualized beings also have the special time, starting today and going into tomorrow, to stay into prayerful watchfulness.

There are the challenges that occur on a daily basis. We are constantly being brought before the false judges. Constantly because of your thoughts, people are condemning you to a crucifixion because the Christ within you is not allowed to move forward.

When you awaken your Christ during challenging conditions, aren't you like the Christ whose on the cross? When things do not happen your way, when you go, "Father, Father, why has Thou forsaken me?" And in your moment of sorrow, like the Roman soldiers, you taste the bitterness as you sigh.

Be crucified with the criminals that you believe live within your heart and soul. And in looking at the imagery of Good Friday, you see the final stage of the Christ Beingness, Jesus, known as the man, as he makes his final transcending moment into a higher plane of consciousness to be finally delivered to humanity. As the Christ, he went through the deepest and darkest challenges within himself, the betrayal of his friends, the denial of his existence by his disciples, and finally, being brought before the masses.

Divine Beingness, the Conscious One, Christ. The people could not see him and condemned him to death. How often on a daily basis do you do this to yourself? I heard your prayers this evening calling out for a blessing, for a healing, for a raising up of your consciousness, and in the inner chambers of your heart, I say you try to hide your anger. The strangers, the ones you don't want to have with you, the ones that crucify the Christ with you on a daily basis. These are the end of the days that Christ spoke about. Your challenge will be second by second.

The one known as Lucifer will be challenging you moment by moment. Making you question, double check and doubt your beliefs. You may ask yourself, "You don't really want to stay on truth." "Look how stupid that person is crossing the street." "Why are they saying that." "Look at that old fool." "Here's so and so on the phone again, going to complain to me, I don't know if I want to hear it." "Uh, listen to the news, did you hear the story about...."

Why are you spending your days, your times, your moments this way? Since every word is a prayer. Why are you spending your time praying for foolishness? Self-examination is important to get to the inner aspect of self. Weeding and separating the wheat from the shaft is important. But to stay as a miller, milling that wheat over and over again until it's no longer usable, is not appropriate for you. These are very tricky times, very tricky times. You as beings are going through the stages of the Cross, going through this time frame, allowing yourselves to see very clearly this Good Friday. This is the night that the blood of Christ poured forth.

You as individuals are pouring forth all the time. Imagine if you were to die this moment. Are you the complete being that you would love to see yourselves to be? Is your heart so clean and open, that as you stand before yourself and witness with your own consciousness all the people you think, say and feel about, will you be comfortable looking at what you have said? Or would you rather put the Christ up for crucifixion so that you would not have to see what's inside yourself? In essence, this is what you do every time, when you go through your challenges. You choose. You have choices every second. Every second, you have choices.

Take the next few days to see your consciousness in stillness, to allow the Earth to be. Do not fumble for the dial to listen for the news but rather play music, sing. Take the time to look at the buds on the trees and be amazed. If your eyes are met with hatred for whatever reason, because someone wants that parking space, or they're judging you because of who you are, hold your head high and your shoulders back and feel the strength of Christ within your being. Looking through them. Looking past them. Looking beyond them and melting them with the strength of love.

If you try and meet them with the strength of hatred, if you try and match their energy of "I'll get you if you get me," then you are acknowledging that evil. If you want to call it Lucifer or Satan, it's right. How many people carry themselves like that? "I'll get even with you." You need to allow yourselves at that point - it goes beyond preaching to others, it goes from within yourself, a dynamic cord, a dynamic string instrument, playing that melody over and over again. Feeling the strings within yourself, melody, melody, melody, melody. Listen and hear yourself. Listen to see if you're out of tune.

And for the next three days, if you can, fast. If you cannot fast, as you eat, eat joyously, seeing the food transforming your body, your being. With the sunrise of Easter, allow yourself to feel the first rays of light hit your body and feel the love come into your heart as you feel your consciousness being uplifted. In the symbolic as well as in the fact that you are no longer going to retain the body forever. But you wish to be the Jesus part of yourself. The man part of yourself. The woman part of yourself. Whether it's Mary, Jesus, that aspect of beingness that is the human connection. Ask that the Christ consciousness within you be awakened. When you do this over the next three days as an initiation for yourself, your thoughts will be amplified a hundred fold.

Now what I have to say, if you travel surround your car in light. Check your tires, your oil. Really check your fan belt. Make sure there's enough air in them. Check the battery. All of you, before you get in that car, bless that car, see it blessed. Make eye contact with no one on the road and see yourselves going and coming back, balanced and healed. Enjoy your life! Seeing family and friends and filled with safety. And if your car needs help, that someone from the highest of the high will be there. So know that you're protected because we feel your fear about your journey. See, there is blessing in everything.

I want to say from the bottom of my heart that there will be some challenges for all of you. But how do spiritual soldiers get tough if they don't go to boot camp? The boot camp is your own mind. That's all you're going to have to challenge. Because things will happen to people around you, but nothing, but nothing will happen to you It's that wanting to run out to rescue. That wanting to protect the one's you love. But understand they're asking for these challenges on some level so that they can return their heart's to Divine Beingness. Why do people do these things? Why do people forget? Request to the blessed Mother, Father, Divine Creator to put them in a beautiful small basket

51

and send them out with flowers into the water. Your offering, your belief that as you ask, so shall you receive. Allow yourselves to see your Angels.

Easter is a time of celebration. Easter is a time when you remember all the Saints, all the Angels. If you cannot see the Christ in the man or the woman standing in front of you, then remember each individual is born as a child, innocent, through a mother in pain. Bringing forth a child out of love. The child may not have been wanted, but once that child is there, there is love. And if you cannot see the Christ in the person that is in front of you, try to remember that that person too is still a child. A child that did not receive the love that it needed in the very beginning of its growth.

What you see on the planet Earth today are human beings that do not know how to love. There can only be hatred when there is a lack of love. That is the worse curse that Satan could fill as a promise to this Earth. When you know this, you will cry as the Angels cry. For what feels better than Love? What pain these people are in to be so filled with anger. They are crying to be loved. You know it's difficult to love a child whose disobedient and unwanted and carrying on. If inside yourself, you cannot do it, then you hand it up to the highest of the high, for this is God's child. You must be honest, for there is not always love in your heart. All you have to say is, " I send this child back to its mother." "I send this child back to its father."

I ask you to take this Easter time and to really take the time to bless and bless and bless yourselves. If you wake up, that's a blessing. If you don't wake up, the game is over! And pray and pray and pray! Spend the next four days praying every time you hear a complaint, pray for ten minutes. You'll be praying all week. You'll see your lives start loosening up, start being more free, and at that point people will become resentful of you because their lives will be hard. They'll want to know what trick it is that you know. Don't try and explain it, just live it!!

What I'm going to do is end. Go in peace and may God be with you!

Tapping Into Serenity/Inner Beingness

Michael: April 15, 1993

I would like you to think of what Serenity is. I would like you to truly understand the word, Serenity. Place your consciousness in Serenity and surrender all of your life's work from the beginning of your consciousness in this lifetime to the present. Place all that turbulence and all of those lessons into the consciousness known as Serenity. The family, yourself, projects, all of it. Even if your life right now feels like one big tangled knot. The goal for you is to pull in and to take that knot and bathe it in the ocean, the tranquillity, the serenity of Love. To make it simple, it's kind of like hair conditioner when your hair is tangled. It creates the same sensation, that softness, that silkiness, that richness, that greatness.

Human beings today have forgotten how to enjoy nature. Even in their efforts of trying to preserve the consciousness of nature, they are worn out from trying to make it happen so other people can enjoy it. People are working so hard at trying to make you enjoy. People are working so hard at trying to raise your consciousness. People are working so hard at trying to knock down your consciousness. Just as you were saying in the meditations, that once you're out of your own stream of consciousness and you try to follow someone else's stream of consciousness, there is turbulence. That's what group mind is all about. Human beings are trying to create a consciousness of turbulence so that you can feel the pain and anger.

Stirring up a pond and making the water muddy does not allow you to drink from that water. It is after all the sediment has dropped, after all the particulate matter has left the water, that the water is clear again. Now you're able to and want to drink the water. No one wants to drink cloudy water. But humanity today wants you to drink a cloudy consciousness. Did you drink today from a cloudy consciousness? How many moments today did you drink deep from your own inner sanctum well of knowing that Divine Beingness is truly in charge of your life? And who is Divine Beingness, but you! The deepest aspect of you that's connected to the Divine Mother, Father, Divine Creator.

You are being given your lessons so that you can appreciate your life force. Did you give thanks for all your lessons today that make your life that much clearer? Or did you question why you had to have so many lessons today? Did you drink from cloudy consciousness or did you drink from the clarity and the serenity of your divine inner beingness. Your clearest cup of water.

Christ said, "Those of you who drink from the cup of water from the river of life will never experience death." "May your mouth fill with water so that you experience this life." What I explained to you today about that water is the same water that Christ talks about. It is the well of your consciousness. It is the water from the well of eternal life.

Now is the time to not be afraid. Now is the time to not wonder, what shall I do next? Where you are now is your highest level of evolution in consciousness! Think about that! This is what you've got! Pretty good stuff, Huh?? This is it. If you were to die right now - bingo, poof, end of the world - this is the level of consciousness you are at. No veil gets lifted with instantaneous knowledge. This is not that van with prizes that is going to pull up and give you more consciousness than your mind is capable of receiving.

There is a phrase on your Earth, "What you see is what you get." This is it! Every moment, every day! I'm trying to emphasize this for a point folks. You have choices to develop your psychic-spiritual capabilities. Or you have the capabilities to develop a world of illusion and to stay focused in on the symptomatic problems that are before you and then you can bang your head against the wall. Banging your head against the wall is not going to make the traffic light change and turn green. Or the spaghetti cook any faster. Or get your term paper done any quicker. Neither will it make you lose weight any faster. Or make your neighbor turn down his music or do anything. Being in a victim state, and saying, "What's the use, I guess I give up." doesn't do anything either. Fretting over children and parents does not make you a good person. It makes you a person who frets. The only thing that should have frets is a guitar. But even the neck of a guitar when it is warped cannot play correctly, so the notes may sound like they're in tune for the moment. But quickly, the tune goes out because the neck is bent. If the neck is bent, then the strings cannot stay taught. Many of you are out-of-tune guitars.

We're coming to a close, like Christ said, "This Earth will pass away, but my words will never pass away." This Earth will pass away. Do you want me to say it again? This Earth will pass away! But the thing is, the Earth will pass away. You will pass away.

Now, let's go over some metaphysical 101 class here. Remember a long time ago when you first started your spiritual path? Today is the last day of your life. Today is the rest of your life. This is the last moment you will ever live. Think about it. If you had no more time left to live, is it worth living your life the way you are now living it? Are you going to die with an exclamation of "Oh !!##~!!"? Or are you going to die with the words of "Oh God", gentle in beauty. Or die with the words of "Oh God.(terror)." Or "Not now!" Or "Oh bleep!"

What is the first thing that you do when something disorganized happens in your life? Do you sit there and go "Oh blessed Divine Light, thank you for this disorganization." Or do you sit there and go, "Oh, mumble, complaint?" How you react and respond today, this moment, this second, to catastrophes is how you are going to react when you make your transition, folks! Do you want to be in fear and leave this plane and enter into the plane of disruption. Your words carry the vibrations of what you feel or say at transition.

This is why we keep saying over and over again. Why do you choose, as individuals, to stay focused in on the lower aspects of yourselves? Why do you choose, when challenges come up, to say, "Oh, this challenge was given to me by God and I don't know how to handle it." Or "Why is God giving me this challenge, I don't understand it." "It's so easy to talk about it but it's hard to do."

So that is your affirmation. That is your instantaneous affirmation. Then when you remind each other that "This is good." "This is wonderful," you're starting to really get it, starting to feel it. Then, you make fun of one another and say, "Oh yeah, right, this is good, hah, hah." That's support? No, that's not support. That is showing your own incompatibility to accept that someone else can grow and to cheer them on. You are examples for one another, yourselves, your family, your friends, your community. You are examples.

A spiritual example can be shown with humor. It can be shown with serenity. It can be shown on many different levels. But the thing is, it doesn't matter what you say you believe in. What really matters is how you take your belief and make it work for you. It doesn't matter if the whole world doesn't like you. What matters is, "Are you true to your beliefs in Divine Beingness?"

You have to remember that not everyone likes anyone whose on the spiritual path. Think back to these simple examples. What did they do to Christ? Okay, that's one example there. Okay, get the big picture? Spiritual beings are not the most sought after people. They are not put up on a pedestal. They are usually put up on a cross! They are usually done away with! So, gee, why do you have so many lessons coming at you? Oh, could it be the darkside trying to get to you? Oh, what a concept. "God's doing this and I don't know why." Well, maybe it's not just God doing this and you don't know why. Maybe it's just the darkside testing you to see how weak your true belief system and spirit are. What a concept! The more struggles that come at you are more lessons and tests.

There is a time, however, when you really become still. When the lessons come at you rapid fire. One after another. You kind of just blaze through them, kind of like a hot knife to butter. It's like, "So what, there it is, I get to keep going, can't let that drag me down!" So, think about that, you want to go into the Sea of Serenity, drink from the well of the water of life and try to remember, even if you have to wear a string on you finger, that help is just a phone call away!

Hear what the person has to say to you. Let the person shake it out. Shout it out. Do what they have to do, then say, "Okay, surround yourself in light." And if the person says, "That's easy for you to say."

Ask them, "What would you rather me say to you then? I'm just here to give you a hand. Your sea is rough. You're on the wrong path. I'm trying to get you out of the water and on to the beach so you can walk to your boat again. So you can get to your path. If you don't want my help, I will hang up now. If I can't convince you, you have to remember yourself."

The purpose to live is for God Realization. That is the only purpose to live. To become God Realized. That is the only purpose to live. The only purpose to live is to become God Realized. That is the only purpose to life. To become God Realized!!

Okay, I will end. Through Divine Light, Divine Love and Divine Wisdom, and so it is.

LAUGH LAUGH LAUGH

Michael: April 23, 1993

Okay, we're going to start this evening. We ask that Divine Beingness and Divine Consciousness come into the room and surround the room with a veil of light so the individuals here may be able to hear the words of wisdom and hear the words of truth that resonate from within themselves and in the Hall of Justice.

The thing that I really need to get across to you tonight is that the heaviness on your planet is only starting. I did tell you that it started increasing so what you are feeling now is nothing. So if it is bothering you now, just pack up and get some Midol. Get whatever you need, because it's going to get worse. So I think it's quite funny that you're concerned at this point. You ain't seen nothing yet, as they say on your Earth. After this year -- oh, I won't tell you about next year. That's for next year. You're going to think this year was fun!!

So the thing is, isn't it great!?! You're making it through every year. Think about it that way. It's like the little kid in the car with the mother and the mother is driving and she knows the journey is eight hours and the little kid keeps asking, "Are we there yet?" "Yes honey, as soon as the next mountain ...." So, it's kind of what's happening with you, "are we there yet?" "No, it's the next mountain." Don't worry about it!

The thing for you to remember and I would like you to do this everyday. I want you to do it twenty, forty or one hundred times a day and its not from the standpoint of me just telling you to do this. You have to change the vibrations surrounding your energies. It is important to get serious. It is important to get intense. It is important

60

to let out vibrations. It is important to do all those marvelous things, but you need to L-A-U-G-H. If you don't do this at least one hundred times a day, you're going to end up looking like shriveled up old prunes coming to class. I don't care what herbs you take, you're becoming the "bitter root". So, the thing is folks, get on the laugh track.

I want to know honestly why you're watching such awful movies. You live in the worse movie there is!! Think about it You're watching not even a shadow of what you're experiencing. It's the culmination of human group consciousness and all of the fears and all of the frustrations and all the power struggles. All of those things now have a platform. Everybody's capability for tolerance is gone. Everybody's capability for understanding has been put in shellac. Everybody's capability for loving even the innocent is over. And you see it yourselves when you see little children walking down the street, six, seven or eight years of age with mean angry looks in their eyes because they are imitating the adults. It's not that the children themselves are mean and angry. They are still children. But they're imitating the adults and the adults are the adults.

Now what's happening here is that individuals and personalities are clashing left, right and center. Who are they clashing with? Themselves!! Every personality is clashing with themselves. You do it with yourselves. You were talking about it tonight. You do it with yourself. You clash with yourself. You become that angry young person inside of yourself.

The Divine Consciousness within a humane aspect of a being has to be developed. We talked about this a long time ago. The humane aspect of the consciousness has to be developed. What is happening when you feel yourself getting angry and frustrated? You need to understand the part of that frustration and anger that you're feeling. Especially when you're looking at what's going on around you. It's very difficult for you to believe as a human being, sitting and working on your own spirituality, that other humans could go so far out of their way to hurt themselves. These are the same brothers and sisters that you're going to see on the other side, on other planes, the same brothers and sisters. This is what's really causing the frustration for you as individuals.

So the thing that you have to remember is when you get into the heavy critiquing (it's very difficult because you're in the human form) you have to remember the human consciousness is very finite. You can vent. Venting is important, but you have to understand, through you as an individual, as a representative of spiritual truth, the acceptance the love and guidance has to be strong and unswerving. It can't waiver. But self-induced punishment for a crime of what someone else is doing is unforgivable. On this planet Earth, the justice system, all your systems are going to fall apart because its not that justice isn't being done. What is happening is that the rules and regulations are changing away from the code of ethics of Divine Spirituality.

The rules of karma are not being handled properly. Even the Old Testament from the Bible is not being followed through. The Testament from the Koran, the Testament from the Native Americans; none of these truths are being adhered to. If someone steals, then they must make reparation. If someone kills, there is no reason to kill. Anger over mistreatment of anyone is not reason to kill. Thou shalt not kill. Thou shalt not covet thy neighbors goods. There's never a good reason to steal. Thou shall never take the name of thy Lord in vain. There's no good reason for anyone to think that anyone has any right to call his or herself a divine teacher of truth, a reverend and take the name of the name of God for your own personal, political or financial gain. There are many men of the cloth out there molesting children, stealing, inciting hatred within communities. They are the Pharisees. They are the ones who are not the representation of God. If you look in your Bible, when Moses came in, the Pharisees were directing the Pharaoh. So it is the lower state of consciousness of human beingness which has yet to establish itself in the physical form.

So what you are seeing is that the very base aspect of humanity has to manifest itself before humanity says how much is too much. And this is why its important for you to <u>Laugh</u>, <u>Laugh</u>, <u>Laugh</u> because the only groups you are going to be able to connect with are the groups that are still light enough to communicate one on one. So that if you did have to rebuild civilization, you would know how to reach out to different cultures, different tribes or different peoples. So that you as individuals whether you are with or without your families, can go and re-establish order. Because there will be fundamentalists and individuals who will be fighting it out on a political level. There will be those individuals who will be pulling it together from spiritual insight. It is important that you laugh and laugh because they will recognize you by the light in your eyes. Walk down the street tomorrow and look in the eyes of people and see how many people whose light is out. You'll recognize them by the light in their eyes.

And if you're so focused in on the garbage you see on television (do not watch television folks, do not watch the news. I beg you for your own safety, do not watch the news.). I told you a long time ago that there is a frequency on that television and you laugh and sometimes you laugh at the wrong things, folks. You can do what you

63

want and you have a free will. But the thing I have to say to you is communication. If you want to read because there's a charge, don't. For your own sake. Read technical books. Read books on herbs. Read other things that will fill yourself with knowledge. Now is not the time to follow the mundane, bogus news. Now is the time to follow the teachings of inner spirit as never before. The news does not make history. History is made by people and events. Unfortunately, the history and events are being chartered by individuals that are only showing you portraits of events that they wish for you to believe is true. This is part of the brain washing process. Key works being flashed over and over again. Do not watch the news. But that is up to you.

What I'm going to do is end because I think I've said enough. Talk about what I've said and think about it. Through Divine Light, Divine Love and Divine Wisdom and so it is.

The God/Goddess Nature Within

Michael: May 6, 1993

In Divine Beingness, Divine consciousness, I ask that the Light and the Truth enter into the room creating the colors of light, creating space for the inner temple to work within each and every person. We ask that the Christ presence enter into the room creating protection and honoring the Highest of the High.

With the intensity in the beginning and the intensity in the end, conflict and resolution, you as individuals on this planet Earth are caught in a myriad of desire, myriad of energies that pull at you from every direction. As children, you used to walk into the fun house and into the hall of mirrors. As a child, you usually could not find your way out by yourselves. You'd laugh. You'd bump into walls and maybe some of you were filled with excitement. Some of you were a little frightened. And what is it in the fear of seeing your reflection in so many different places? What is it that causes the confusion that when you see yourself in so many places you don't know where the entrance is? You don't know where the exit is. You don't know where the path begins.

You as individualized beings of truth here on the planet Earth see fragments of yourself throughout your lives. And in visualizing your lives and looking at yourself from all different directions sometimes you feel fear. Sometimes you feel shame. Sometimes you hope that maybe someone can't really see deep into your heart to understand what's going on inside of you. And sometimes you look at yourself and you laugh. And sometimes in investigating yourself and looking at the different aspects of the life you created, you get lost.

You forget your path. You forget who you are. You forget what reflection you're looking at. Are you looking at yourself or are you looking at someone else? In looking at yourself from all the different directions, from all the different angles, you must allow yourself to take a deep breath and really take a look at what you are seeing. What you are witnessing is an individualized aspect of the Goddess/God nature.

You as beings have to become so immersed in understanding that the truth that emanates from the innermost aspect of your soul, your heart, your being, your mind, your body. The truth that emanates is alive and well and living in every single cell of your body as you sit here today. The God/Goddess energy that you know is giving you life at this moment today. The life-giving prana. The breath that you take, that sustains you, is the breath of God. Can you understand the concept that it is not just oxygen that you are breathing? You are breathing in the aspect of the God creativity, the God/Goddess nature that knows you as an individualized self. As an offspring of the Beloved, you need to breath deep of the breath of God.

You as individualized beings, as you walk on the Earth and you nourish yourself, are eating the fruits and the nectars of the gods. Do you approach your foods that you are eating as the nectar of the gods? It is the life sustaining force and even though this is the world of illusion within the illusion, the creation itself and everything that lives has the life force of God within it. Do you choose to eat the life force of God and sustain yourself with the life force of God. Or do you sustain yourself with the synthetics of man?

You must ask yourself on a daily basis to renew and re-awaken the God/Goddess energy within you. You must partake of what the God/Goddess has provided you. Do you drink water? Water is the blood, the life force of the Earth. The Earth as the Goddess Mother Nature opens her veins willingly as rivers and streams whose heart lovingly pumps life back into you. Or do you allow yourself to drink from the synthetics of man?

When we speak of diet, we know that some of you as individuals still eat meat. You know that as individuals you still eat things that do not help you live in a healthful way and what we are suggesting is that you may want to try just for a week to eat only things that are alive and well. See if you can eat things that you do not have to kill. If you were not to kill anything you would eat nothing at all. But if you were to, as an individual, sustain the least amount of pain upon the aspect of God that is giving up its life for you to live, to heal, to nurture, would you eat plants or would you eat fruit or would you eat seeds? Would you feel because they are of a lesser consciousness that they hold a lesser state in the consciousness of God? If you are to kill a living thing that has eyes, ears, mouth, a mother and father, and to eat of this life, you must give thanks to the spirit who has given its life not so willingly.

You need to ask yourself on a daily basis, when you get out of your bed and you step on your floor and you take a deep breath, or when you hear your alarm if you give thanks to Divine Beingness for providing you with the air to breath? For a heart so wonderful it sustains you during the night. With a mind so perfect that it controlled all of your bodily functions so that you didn't have to put one thought to them? Did you give thanks, as soon as you wake up, to the heat that your body provided to warm you in your bed? To make you so comfortable? Did you thank your bones as you feel the aches and pains, and ask if they can be healed by an adjustment or exercise to make them limber? In the morning when you wake up, if you are sustained by illness and it has crept through your body, did you give thanks to God that you have another day, and the opportunity to live out this pain, to work through your lessons, to move through your life? And as you take your first deep breath, do you give thanks? Period!!

And as you lay your bones down at the end of the night, did you bless your enemies? Many times your enemies are in your mind. They may be screaming at you from your television? They may be screaming at you through your newspaper. Through your radio. You have options. You can believe them. You can bless them. You can let them go. But you create enemies for yourself every day inside of your own mind. How you feel about yourself. You as individualized beings of the God/Goddess nature. Did you see yourself as the God/Goddess who you truly are today?

When you stepped into that shower, into that bath did you feel like the divinity, releasing the energies, through the sacred baptismal water? Did you feel the energy drain from your body that you do not need to carry? And as you anoint yourself with the sacred oils and creams, as you dry yourself with the towel, do you feel the honor? And as you dress yourself do you see yourself dressed in the finest robes? And as you put on your rings and your jewelry, do you see it as part of the ornate apparel that you choose to present yourself as that God/Goddess today?

And as a male, did you see the God within you? Did you feel that center? Did you feel that power? Did you see your sacredness? Did you see the sacredness in the other Goddess as she walked past you?

As individualized beings who are working on your way towards truth, do you see that Goddess, that God, who is here on this Earth connecting with Divine Beingness. Eternal now. Eternal mind. Do you feel it shine forth or do you shrink when you see the sons and daughters of man who will not honor the God that exists within them.

We are not talking about arrogance, we are talking about honor. We are not talking about timid people. We're talking about strength. There's a difference between a knowingness, a lovingness and an individual who feels they have nothing to offer.

What I'm going to ask you to do this week, if you can, if you need to do it with symbols or with statues, is to take the time to really see that you are a God/Goddess on this Earth. Feel the kingdom, feel the charge you have over the Earth as promised to you. Feel your word being your command. Listen to how you as an individual throw away your power and if you hear it being thrown about. Your words are your servants. What do your servants provide for you? Are your servants gathering the richness, the opulence, prosperity and health and life and home and heart. Or are your words imprisoning you into a kingdom that is poor? Filled with servants who are unruly and do as they will. Kill the king, kill the queen, mask the God, mask the Goddess. Unleash yourself from your prison.

Humankind would like you to not see that aspect. There are individuals in power right now that would like to think that they are in power over you. Will you give them that power that they're asking that you hate one another. Will you give them the power that they're asking for you to be afraid of them? Because they cannot see the God/Goddess energy within themselves, does not mean that you cannot see the God/Goddess energy within them. But they are asleep. They are filled with self. They are filled with the nonsense of man. Anoint yourselves. Honor yourselves. And really return your kingdom, your life to the path of the Highest of the High.

Every word and I repeat, every word is a prayer. You are the High Priestess. You are the High Priest. You have been working towards this for life times. Claim your power, claim your rightful place, then you can take your friends, your brothers and sisters, your family by the hand and lead them. You can lead them back into their own proper placement with their own throne, their own crown, their own knowingness, their own honor and dignity. But if you choose to get wrapped up into the nonsense of man you will not be able to lead them anywhere, for you are the one who will be lead.

Take the time this week, if you can, to bless this, to honor this. And when you see friends and you see yourself honoring the false idols of man, pinch yourself, awaken yourself. Place yourself in the proper placement that you deserve. You are part of the Celestial, not part of the earthbound.

With this I end and through Divine Light, Divine Love and Divine Wisdom and so it is.

Tuning In To The Higher Consciousness

Michael: May 20, 1993

In the first place, what I want to say is, humans can fly to the moon but they still can't see God. They can go to the bottom of the ocean but they still can't see God.

What you have to understand is, all of these examples of children playing with toys shows you the loneliness and the incapability that human beings have to utilize their minds to create. It starts out from a simple-hearted, kind-hearted individual creating more comfort and balance for individuals. And what happens? This information turns and is exchanged for more treachery that comes out of the human heart.

What I have to say to you is that the Ancients, the Tibetans and others still have machinery and still have computer information that will be locked in their halls. Locked in their caves. Locked away with the high priests and high priestesses never to be shown to this Earth until humanity has reached and has evolved to a point that it can use these vessels, these vehicles, these utensils for good. This is why Tesla destroyed his machinery. He knew how to take energy out of the atmosphere by using energy grids, tapping into a higher energy form and utilizing this energy for free. But upon seeing how volatile this energy was, when it rocked the entire five or six blocks in Manhattan in the early 1900's, he quickly destroyed this information so that humanity would not go in to a mode of self-destruct. And there are Ancients that are constantly governing, constantly taking information, securing it and locking it away so that mankind, humankind does not create full destruction upon itself.

The thing that I want to say tonight is that you not to get so caught up upon the love-heartedness that humanity creates for itself. But rather allow yourselves to pull back. Pull back and allow yourself to say, "Okay, I know of these things and I choose not to use things." Or, "I know these things and I will use a few of these things." Or, "I know of these things and I will use them anyway because I don't care." Or, "I know of these things and I will not use them because I care." Whatever it is that you say to yourself, stay true to what you feel about that which you hear. However, do not get so emotionally involved that you too forget that inherently, you are a brother, a sister of Divine Light and Divine Beingness. And in order to understand human nature you must experience your own human nature. In order to understand humanity and to raise the human consciousness within yourself, you must see how consciousness within the human form moves, shifts and changes.

You go from the shadowy side of self to the most brilliant aspect of self and you need to allow yourself to see during this time of turbulent flux, turbulent change, that if you cry out for God, God's presence is there. If you cry out for the Christ, you are crying out for the consciousness that is within yourself. And you have to constantly remember that the second coming of Christ has been said to be the coming of the Christ consciousness that is within you. The physical manifestation of Christ can be seen by anyone. But the physical knowingness of the Christ energy can only be known by a few.

So it is better that you as an individual awaken, unlock, release, unsheathe, unshield and expose that Divine higher archial energy that flows from within yourselves and try to the best of your capability not to allow your ego to pour forth. But allow the God aspect to pour forth into all situations and when life feels like a barren desert to allow yourselves to see that that barren desert had once been an ocean. Go back into your mind's memory and remember when it was an ocean. An ocean of love. And when you see a barren desert you allow yourself to look upon this and say, "This too is part of the creation." And then allow yourself to continue your journey forward getting towards your own oasis. Because in many ways, many times, many shapes and many fashions that is what life may seem to be at this moment in time, one large desert.

But because you have that lighted consciousness of the Christ, of the Buddha, of the Krishna, of the Om, of the I Am, of the One who has no name, you as individuals in Truth, you as individuals in Light, you as individuals in Beingness, like Moses, will receive manna from the sky. You will not be forsaken in this desert consciousness that exists on the planet Earth today.

You must surround yourself constantly with friends, friends, friends who are of the light. Friends, friends, friends who are there to support you. Brothers and sisters, individuals that you recognize in the streets walking. Allow yourself to recognize the Divine Light within them by bowing your head and giving a smile, or moving your hand just to signify, to notify that you see them too as part of the humanness that walks upon the Earth.

You need to understand that the so called political powers and the so called negative, darker energies that surround the planet are just really winding out their time. You've seen many cowboy movies where the sheriff is moving in on the bad cowboys and there they are all sitting in the house talking about how they're going to blast their way out but they're surrounded by the sheriff and there's no way they can get out.

They still shoot and there's casualties back and forth and the guys in the house usually get shot to pieces and no one makes it through. Occasionally someone does make it through and then everybody cheers because the bad guys are safe. Its hard to tell who the bad guys are anyway. It's kind of a conditioning to show that bad is good and good is really not so good.

But when you as individuals are in that movie house of consciousness and you see the bad guys, just surround and circle them. Instead of with a posse, surround and circle them with the Apostles or with the positive aspects within yourself and say, "And this too comes from Spirit and it is of the Light. And if it is of the shadow may it return back into the nothingness from where it came." So when you're bad, understand that bad is bad, And you can say, "Okay this is not part of the aspect that I'd like to project. I accept it. I acknowledge it. I see what is for what it is. I'm not going to cover it up, make it better, make it shine in the different way. It is what it is."

And what happens when you shine light directly upon a shadow? It goes away. So the thing is, you as individuals in truth, are not unlike the light that you can put on that shadow. I want you to do as an experiment on the next sunny day to try and get rid of your shadow. You cannot. You can watch it expand as it gets longer, you can watch it shrink as it gets shorter, but if you look, that shadow will be there And so will the darkness that's with you. So will that so-called ignorance that's within you. So will that so-called negativity that's within you. So will that so-called part of your psyche or consciousness.

As long as you are human, you are a shadow cast upon the Earth trying to capture the reflection of God and trying to see yourself of God and to have that light shine from within. But until then you are just but a shadow of the Divine Beingness, and in essence, this is why all beings in truth are also beings in untruth.

So you need to reconcile with yourself first the "us" against "them" syndrome. It is any form of discrimination on any level when you go "us" or "them" because the "them" are still people. The "them" are still you. The "them" of "them" are you. The "them" to you are "them". There are so many "thems" looking at "them". Who is looking at who? It is always you! I don't care how many times you look in the mirror. If you break that mirror and you look at a thousand pieces, which one is your reflection?

So the thing is that you as an individual need to pull back every time you are near to the "them" and understand you have successfully done what the ignorance or the ego, or what some people call the devil, has created inside yourself. You have been able to see the separation of God so clearly that you are willing to call your brethren "them". If you can still do the "them", then how are you ever going to see the One, because the One just is! The "them" are, the One is!

I have a question for all of you. Do any of you see yourself as really working on your spiritual self 100% of the time? No one lie! I thought so! And I shall end. That is your assignment!

Vibrate in on Spirit
Focus on Your Om Points
Michael: June 10, 1993

We give thanks to Divine Beingness and we give thanks to the Christ energy for entering the room this evening.

The thing that I'd like to talk to you about this evening, more than anything else, is of the body aspect or the physical form as you know it. The reason why you will have to put so much energy and effort into creating change in the body is that vibrations are really going to be impactful upon you as people.

As you know, around the Earth right now there are different sound vibrations that are being heard and they are creating for some people a sense of disorientation. We have talked before about the sound that would penetrate the Earth. Some of the sound that is coming to the Earth is a hum that is being heard and felt in different areas around the world. This hum is not coming necessarily from a place that you as individuals know to be the physical plane. It is coming from a higher esoteric aspect or a higher plane of consciousness. The hum is the om point which is reverberating back to the planet.

As we said, as the vibration on this Earth shifts, the different intonations or tones from different fields of vibration are going to be felt on this planet Earth. Some individuals will feel that the energy is coming from the darkside. Some individuals will feel that it is possibly coming from military installations. But the military itself, is not sure where this sound is coming from. What we want to say to you is that the sound is not man made. The sound is coming from different levels, different planes, different aspects, where the energy infiltrates and vibrates into the Earth. So in this sense, if you wish to say it does come from another planetary source, it's coming from the new planet that is being made for those beings who are going to take that evolutionary leap away from the Earth.

You see the Earth itself could possibly be destroyed by this sound that is now being heard around the world. What it is doing is creating a shifting or a changing of the molecular state that is around people. Individuals who are highly sensitive hear this sound and it makes them disoriented.

What that means is that these individuals are operating on a different vibratory level or different frequency than other people. But it is also being heard in mass. So it is not one or two people who are hearing it. And as you become more attuned, you may start hearing the sound in this area. Basically, it's like a hum. It sounds on many occasions as if your ears are ringing, as if coming back from a loud rock & roll concert. It is a ringing in your ears or a humming that goes through your body and it can disorient your thinking process. So you need to stay focused in on Divine Spirit. What you are hearing once again is the sound coming through the different planetary vibrations.

Part of the reason that this sound is penetrating people so is because the vibration is not ringing on the level that it needs to and this is why it is really important that you as individualized beings really vibrate in on Spirit and focus in on the om points of your own. Again to focus in on the om means going deep in the body and aligning the different frequency that you hear or feel. And it is bringing in that om point by using your mind and your voice and taking a deep breath and doing your om when you feel that the vibration frequency is off. So what you are doing is taking the vibration and with the om you change the whole vibrationary field in the room. And if the vibration is on another level, again, you feel the energy. You feel where it is coming from and then you allow yourself to realign it with another om. So you as personality selves, as beings, have the capability when you hear these frequencies to do this.

So you really do need to understand that when I say things are going to manifest on the Earth plane and I give a time frame, usually it will be within that time frame when it has to do with human events. Human events and human consciousness are very easy to see. It is like a play, so to speak, and we see the human drama unfold. We get to read the play and we get to see the end. You have to go through it moment by moment and line by line. We already know how the play is going to end and that the actors and the actresses are all bit part actors. There are no headliners that we can see. You are all doing your bit part and everybody tries to be the head star and the only head star is Divine Consciousness. And until you allow yourselves to grasp that, then this play that you call the play of living is always going to have these uncalculated and calculated moments of deception. But that's all soon coming to an end and you won't have to worry about deception and things of that nature very much longer because the Earth is about to go through massive change.

And that is all I have to say on that. So what I'm going to do is end. I give thanks to Divine Beingness, I give thanks to Divine Consciousness for allowing me to come through once again. We will be speaking to you more than likely for a short while longer and then it is going to be up to you to continue to do the work.

Through Divine Love, Divine Light and Divine Wisdom.

Praying for Others

Michael: June 17, 1993

As you selflessly put out the energies of healing, of blessings toward your fellow human beings: the sincerity, the pain, the heartfelt feelings, the sorrow, all of the encompassing vibrations that resonate in your innermost core being, we are working with you to lift and transform these energies to create balance, love, serenity and joy.

It is as if you are warriors that have had a long and hard battle with the enemy. You come back weary and tired from trying to protect what you hold to be true. It is the land of love. The land of infinite wisdom that you are trying to protect. At a certain juncture you will finally recognize within yourself that the enemies you are fighting only have power because you give them power. This is not to say a discouraging word. Not at all.

It is truly a very difficult thing to have simplicity, total love and understanding as the calling card in the human consciousness. But all of you are trying so intensely on a moment by moment basis. You are all working so very, very hard. We truly plead with you as human beings in the physical form to try and relax and enjoy your lives. It is truly the time to take the scissors to the ties that bind you, the thoughts that stop you, the fear that cripples you and the anger that can consume you. In matters of family, you want to say it is healed and it is done. It just takes time for the earthly beings to resonate with the highest vibration from Divine Consciousness.

As that energy filters into the physical plane, the human beings body may not be totally receptive to the higher vibratory frequency. So it takes awhile for the human body, the human psyche, the human being, the consciousness to actually absorb the message, the lesson, and embrace the Love and Truth. Know that on a higher level that it is done. Within the physical form, the forms beyond your spirit forms the different planes of consciousness that you dwell in, because you are still unaware, you're not consciously activating those planes. But you still have energy there. You still have access to the information there. You still have a potential to be there. And remember, because you are working on yourself, at times you can actually access this life. So in times when you are praying for sons and mothers and daughters whose vibration is not that of one who is seeking the truth, be gentle with yourself. The body cannot attune itself to the vibration. But on a higher level, a true desire is to be in alignment with God.

The higher intention is to be vibrating in love. The black in the human consciousness hears the unknown in the transitory time called death because it does not understand in the finite consciousness that it has been there before. And also understand the hammering. The hammering of pain. The hammering of suffering. The hammering of anger. The hammering is sometimes abuse of the body, through dependencies. It is the only way the psyche knows to break down the barriers in order to set itself free. Many of those you have prayed for cannot even hear what is being said to them because of the hammering, the demolition, the change and transformation.

We are trying to be encouraging to those of you who are suffering in pain, emotionally and psychologically because you see the potential of the family and friends of the Earth. We have compassion for you because you do pray. We say now is the time to pull back, offer your prayers, cut the ties and know that it is time.

This is the time that was spoken of, and know that their highest potential, if it is not met in this incarnation will be met at another time. And it is because of your prayers and your belief in seeing the light within them that helps create this situation to take a rapid growth towards reclaiming their Godhood. It may be difficult because of the emotional attachments to your family to step back, but when you feel you know how to create the change, pull back, take a deep breath, pray and allow yourself to go out and enjoy your life. And give thanks, because you were on the same path and the same road that they are now at. You were once there yourselves. And so you know the beautiful outcome when a vision is held inward and so it is.

Healing

Michael: September 21, 1993

In the first place we want to talk many different things.

You are going into a very powerful vibration. In understanding aspects of the occult comes a tremendous amount of responsibility. You are learning some of the lighter aspects of power. In future times, in the next few weeks to follow, you will be learning about more powerful ways of healing. In learning about healing and raising peoples vibrations and energies you must always keep in your consciousness the karma involved in healing. If a person is not meant to be healed, please remember, you will not heal them. You will accelerate their illness and their death process. That is part of the karmic obligation of true healers. To heal an individual from the standpoint of personal satisfaction is an ego situation.

Individuals that come in full faith and truth know that they wish to move forward and learn more of their lives. Their healings are permanent. Individuals whose lives have come to an ending, for whatever reasons, the healing will assist them in their process of transition. Individuals who are coming because they do not want to work on anything and they are just tired of being in pain, then you can only just facilitate a temporary healing of their pain.

So there are many different things that you are going to get involved in. But vibrationally now, let's talk about the now, the moment you are in. The planet cannot handle the energy of the Earth right now. Universal direction and vibration and healing of this planet is at a pinnacle. You are at the zenith, right now.

All of your personal intention must be on healing yourself and healing your own lives. You have to understand that during this transitory time that individuals, personality selves, as they come to the awakening process, will start seeing themselves merge back into the Godhead. Individuals whose personal prices have been about personal development and destructive development and control and ego and attitude will feel so far away from the Godhead that they will be crushed internally by their own lack of spiritual understanding. Many, many, many more people as the process speeds up, will be dying of various diseases and many more catastrophes are about to hit your planet.

You as individuals and personality selves need to continuously stay open to Divine Light and Divine Beingness. You may use your rituals. You may use your prayers. You may use your healing capabilities. But understand that you need to stay totally prepared and you must really be on guard and say to yourself, "I could die at any moment. Why should I waste my time on this situation? Is this situation really worth me getting cancer over by being so worried? Is this situation really worth my health in holding on to it?"

You are being given tests. And as a support network, you need to work with one another to move these obstacles out of your path. You do not need to come down with disease, illness or death in order to move through these situations. Bodies will start feeling pain in places that you have never experienced before.

With the third eye re-awakening and with your metaphysical body really taking hold, you will feel odd shakes, strange vibrations, lightening and a dizzying. And almost a swooning as you stand. You are not to waste your time on the UFO sightings and alien sightings that are happening now. You are not to waste your time with the brainwashing of the make believe changing of governments, the make believe signing of treaties, the make believe financial debts, the make believe wars and the make believe threats by individuals, groups or countries.

And there is a good reason why I say this is all make believe. The powers that be and not the powers from the White Brotherhood are manipulating humankind. Through the power of television, radio, film and broadcast they are fabricating stories at such a phenomenal rate that the human consciousness is brainwashed to the point of dullness and inaction. It is triggered by fear and reinforced by hatred. And the very laws that the Ancients had set down as discipline are now gone.

There are those of you who adhere to the old laws, the only laws, the true laws. The new world order is the satanic bible manifest on the physical plane. The anti-Christ will reveal itself to humanity shortly. You will see through the human skin and you will see the anti-Christ. The anti-Christ must not see you. So you must learn very, very, very, very intently to be invisible, to be centered, protected and surrounded in love.

So as the time draws nearer, the stakes get higher and you will be pushed to the test even more. So it is up to you to remain the victorious and the victor over the negativity of the darkside. So have fun this Winter and Fall and learn truths. I will come back again and so it is.

To a Linear Path

Michael: December 14, 1993

Some of the things I want to discuss with you this evening are not things that are going to be earth shattering, even though the Earth is shattering. But the things I have to say to you this evening are more for you to look at. To look where you as an individual, you as a personality self are truly headed.

You need to imagine, just for this one split moment in time that your life is a map. That your body and your mind is a vessel and you are on course. To what? What do you find yourself focused in on? Are you focused in on going in a big circle? There are many people in this room tonight that I see focused in on circular energy. Thinking the same thought, making a wider and wider pass, but going in the same circle that I've seen you going in for the last 100,000 years.

Okay, but you are getting bigger. It's almost like Haley's Comet. You're making an approach every seventy years to the same spot. What I am asking you to do tonight is nothing revolutionary. The thing is, you as individualized selves have got to look at your maps, look at your course and make a decision tonight. "Will I break this circular habit and will I allow myself to go in a linear and direct path to God realization? Or am I to forever to be shopping in the malls of my mind?"

You have an opportunity tonight to stop looking for a discount and stop looking for a bargain and go straight to an expensive store. So the thing is, you have got to ask yourselves, "Am I worthy of divine revelation, worthy of God/Goddess consciousness? Am I worthy of leaving all of the mundane behind and moving in an upward motion, going beyond the teachers that I see, beyond the Dalai Lama, going beyond the finite form and reaching the infinite?" How many of you get stuck when I said Dalai Lama? The whole class! But you are doing great. Who pulled the emergency switch. The thing is, even the Dalai Lama had to start somewhere, okay? He had to start in his rudimentary form being born into the human form working through lifetimes and lifetimes of karma to achieve this lifetime form. Working within this lifetime framework trying to teach light and forgiveness. Teaching peace and harmony in a world that is jaded and a world that has become hard. A world where children have no dreams. A world where nightmares enter into the hearts of those who have just left the higher planes of consciousness to manifest in the human form forgetting where they come from.

You are individuals who have left higher consciousness and entered into human form and are now striving back to have just a small memory of where you have been and where your destiny is to be. So I want to say to you very seriously this evening, that when you meet on the twenty first, I truly want you to make an effort between now and then to have at least five minutes of your life dedicated, focused in on only the Highest of the High. Not dwelling on what you are incapable of doing. Not dwelling on what you have not achieved. Not focusing in on the people who are hurting you. Not thinking about the furniture you do not have. Or the weight you haven't achieved. Or the relationship that you are not in yet. But focus in on the light relationship that you are in within yourself, within the Christ, within the Goddess, within God.

Focus on all of that energy within you, the power and the strength, the wisdom and all the fortitude that it would take for you to overcome limitation and mountains and mountains of trouble. It is between you and a thought that separates you from a revelation of God. It is just a thought. Think about it. It's just like a mirror. It's a thought. Your mirror is reflecting your consciousness. Your finite soul is right now reflecting your finite consciousness. Here is your consciousness and the Divineness that is within you. The only thing stopping you is a thought and that thought is, "I can't." A thought, one measly, tiny, thin framework. Something thinner than cellophane, finer than a thread, as weak as a piece of lint is preventing you from understanding who you truly are within yourself. But you make that lint as if it were a plank. You make the cellophane into a form that is stronger than titanium. You take these thoughts and you make them of a strength of bars of a prison that no one could escape. And when I say it is that simple, I am not lying. I am telling you the truth.

So next time you are having this feeling that, "I can't. Where is God? I've been forgotten. My life is a shambles. Look at me. Oh poor me. I'm alive. What a consolation prize! I'm supposed to be happy that I'm here?" But then I tell people it beats the alternative. What is the alternative? You are in an endless cycle of life, death and rebirth. You are in the karmic wheel of the never ending wheel of karmic misfortune. You just need to know that you are. That you are the "I AM" And you see it and you say it, but you don't believe it.

We don't know what type of jet fuel you need, but we will tell you this, didn't it feel good when it was cold outside the other day and you knew you had plenty of food in your home? It is that kind of a sensation and feeling knowing that when you are prepared to meet

Divine Beingness, when that God light shines upon you, you will not be trembling when you come face to face with the face of God, but you will be humbled.

Be open. Be loving and be receptive because we really say to you that this season you will feel things you never felt. You will see things you have never seen before. But all you are seeing is what has always been, will always be and open to anyone.

I'm going to end but I want you to think about those things and I say it in jest but I mean it with all sincerity. So when you come together, really come together as one thought, one word, one heart and one action. And when you meet the man, woman and child of the street, you light their candle from the light within yourself and as you bow your head, see your light move into them so that they may see the light that glows within themselves. You are all part of the Divine chain of consciousness. Allow yourself to become a stronger link. Don't allow yourself to become a weaker one. And so it is.

Speaking Your Truth

Michael: December 21 1993

Divine Beingness, we ask that the Christ Consciousness come through this being into this room so that you can hear the voices of the Angels. We ask that the room be surrounded by Light, by Truth, by Wisdom. We ask that all the Angels in the hierarchy make manifest themselves this night.

In the first place, we want to give thanks for your sincerity and your effort in order to attempt to raise forth the higher energies of Spirit. As you know, at this particular moment in time, the Earth is at its lowest ebb that consciousness has ever felt. We want to say that by you praising Divine Beingness and by you praising the Earth, in your efforts to create an awareness and an opening, you add to those energies of those people who are on the Earth and in the Earth today. Those people who are trying to pray from the bottom of their hearts to create a spiritual awareness so the Earth, as she goes through her inner awakening, does not have to labor so long in her childbirth of consciousness.

You as individualized beings of self, this evening, during the Solstice, have been receiving many blessings, told and untold. This evening as you sit and celebrate with one another, in your sincerity and in your solemnness, in your joy, in your peace and in your tears, we ask you to be honest. We ask you not to hold back. And we ask you to speak what is on your mind. Tonight, in this room, if truth is spoken, revelations will be unfolded to you within.

If you are too embarrassed to speak your heart, then you must ask yourself what really lives within you. If you see your words come out like a dagger, make mental note of this. It means your Christ within needs to be awakened.

You also need to observe the children that live inside your being. How to raise them up. How to see them on high. Understand that it is the awakening and the birth time of the Christ consciousness. Understand it is the awakening and the birth of all spiritual consciousness. Understand it is the awakening and the birth of the Angels. Understand the trumpets have been blasted. Understand the seals have been broken. Understand you are in the time of revelation. Understand the stars will fall from the sky. Understand you will soon receive light bodies. Allow yourselves to enjoy this evening. Allow yourselves to celebrate.

In the coming weeks we are going to ask you to go out into the fields and out into the forests and do Ceremony as it is meant to be done.

Through Divine Light, Divine Love and Divine Wisdom we gave thanks and so it is.

Prayer

Michael: January 11, 1994

In the first place, I'd like to welcome all of you and thank all of you once again for sharing and being of witness to the events of the Earth as they unfold. We want to tell you that what you will be experiencing is no different than what you have been discussing in this room.

It is very interesting to observe the different visions, viewpoints and aspects of the presence of the God-mind active, alert and working within each and everyone of you. You all have a different perspective on what your own personal reality is. You all have a different perspective on what you believe God to be.

What I can tell you is that you must pray. This is nothing different than I've told you over the years. You must pray like you've never prayed before! You must pray like you have never prayed before! You must pray like you have never prayed before! Understand that you can take that word "pray" two ways. Either you can pray. PRAY to God. Or you become prey. PREY to the darkside. It is up to you as individuals whether you choose to be stalked or you choose to be a stalk, strong and tall, representing the Divine acting in your eternal radiance, acting in your eternal essence. Being as a flower in the field or you can be stalked and prey for other than the Highest of the High.

You have to understand that your mind will be torn in two different directions at the same time over the next six months. The only way you are going to create a balance and a center for yourself is to

91

pray. That is the inner foundation for your spiritual dwelling. That is going to be the water that nurtures your thoughts. That is going to be the fuel that produces the energy to allow your body to be motivated and to move.

The energies on the planet are going to get heavier and heavier and heavier. You are going to feel as if people are being held down from now until March or April. Very heavy, heavy, heavy feelings. You as individuals, on the other hand, can allow yourselves to rise up from that heaviness and never allow yourselves to even touch that heaviness and be in an elevated state of beingness.

Humanity as a whole has gone absolutely crazy. You witness it everyday. As some of you have pointed out this evening. You are connecting with that God-force within those who are studying metaphysics and spirituality. It is extremely important that you never forget that you are human. But it is <u>extremely important</u> that you never forget that you are God. It is better to remember that you are God first, then human. It is better than to focus in on your human dilemma and then rapidly tumble into the pits of desire. The physical plane as it dissipates before your very eyes, as the world changes before your very eyes, as governments change before your very eyes as laws change before your very eyes as your freedom gets taken away before your very eyes and as you become slaves to the government before your very eyes, you had better stay focused in on God.

All human dignity is being stripped away! Do you think it is by coincidence that there are all these horrible shows on television? It is to wipe away your human dignity, my dears. Do not bother yourself with such filth! Do not even bother to discuss the filth of humanity at the dinner table of God. But rather clean yourselves internally.

Disregard that which is below you. Disregard your animal aspects of self. Understand it is there, so you can recognize it when you see it in other humans. But allow yourselves to focus in on God. This is how the Masters operate my friends. They see beyond the human exterior and they truly connect the God within. From there they can take that God energy within and bring it into the emotional, into the ethereal, into the subtle planes and finally into the physical creating a healing. They have tapped into the inner workings of that person, moving through all the different layers of the gross physical, ethereal and spiritual planes which are not yet connected totally with the God-head And they bring that energy through, creating a healing, drawing that energy out, energy that was already within. That is why the Masters can walk through the jungles and the animals do not attack them. For when they look deep into the eyes of the animal, they activate the presence of the seed of God within them, thereby neutralizing their animalistic fear. For they cannot even feel the animal aspect within the Masters, they can only feel the presence of Love! And this is what you need to generate. You may not necessarily become a Master within the year, but you must practice and act and feel yourselves to be in the presence of the Master. You must try and emulate the Master so that you as individualized beings, as the world shifts and changes before your very eyes, you still have your footing very strongly in your spiritual truth.

Because of all these so-called politically correct things which are happening, human beings are turning into little robots so that they no longer are allowed to have thoughts. Though no one should hate anyone or to tell someone that they could be jailed for thinking incorrectly is the darkside in the disguise of God working. God would not jail you for disliking someone or thinking the wrong way. God gives you an opportunity to create change and balance within yourself. Through forced change comes anger. Through the forced anger comes violence. Through violence comes destruction. And then the very tools that are being used to stop separation creates more separation than ever existed since the beginning of human beingness.

Stay focused on God. What you are about to see on the planet you will never see again. Stay focused in on Spirit and only align with those who are of the Highest of the High. Think about those things. Think about those things and pray about those things. And so it is.

Opening To The Truth Within

Michael: February 22, 1994

I give thanks this evening for being able to come into this room and into the vibration that you are all sitting in.

You will feel the power of my voice and my words but allow yourselves to open up to your own truths. You need to understand that the way that you feel this moment is from an energy and vibration that you are able to tap in to at any moment.

The world and its illusion, the human beings and their leaders, whether religious, spiritual or political are all speaking of their varying levels of truth. The only leader you need is the leader within yourself. It may feel good to hear my words. It may feel good to hear other teachers of truth. The reason it feels good is that it activates the vibrating force from within your being that already exists. It is fine tuning the knowledge from within yourself.

When I speak of the Earth changes I am drawing in from the Universal Mind and God's consciousness. The reason that you so readily accept my words is that it vibrates with the truth within yourself. I do not make things happen. They are already being revealed and have already occurred.

You are seeing the movie after it has been written. This is why it is so difficult for human beings to understand that this is the world of illusion. What you see before you in your realm is an illusion. Even the words that you hear are sonic sounds of illusion. What you are feeling is the truth force that radiates. We must use words because you cannot sensitize yourselves enough, except within the deepest form of meditation, to feel the vibration of truth. When you are feeling truth,

95

you are absorbing truth. Words are meaningless. And this is why we say that if you are going to speak, understand that you are formulating from the ethers, like with clay, to create within your reality either a prayer to elevate you to the Highest of the High or a prayer that will encase you in the lowest of the low.

The world of illusion shifts, shapes and changes. Do not try to scrutinize too intensely the actions of others. Use the magnifying glass on yourselves. Do not waste this valuable time caring about any of the things you are doing. Rather utilize the time for experiences in learning and understanding. As I have said before, the things you do are the commercial breaks in your life. The movie begins when your focus in on God. The movie continues when you realize that all around you is a show. When you get wrapped up in the show, you are stuck in the commercial, the meaningless part of your life.

In being human it is very difficult to transcend your emotions. However, if you can use your mind as a watchdog to say, "Okay, I'm really keyed up in this right now. I really believe that this is important but in essence it's just busy work that I'm doing. Am I radiating the truth? Am I enlightening others as I pick up this piece of garbage or am I showing arrogance because I'm picking up the garbage?" Or is it, "Oh here is something that needs to be removed and placed over here. It's just in my way. It's no big deal. I'll move forward because it is meaningless."

We're not saying to be without emotion and to act in a state of tranquillity as if you were medicated. We are talking about when to raise your voice, when to get excited and when to let it go. You do not need, even for a moment, to endanger your health by being so concerned about the health and welfare of others. To be an effective teacher, to be an effective student, to be an effective healer is to stand unswerving in the eye of God knowing that but by the grace of God go you.

The events around you are none of your business, none of your concern. If you can lend a hand, fine. If you can learn something, fine. If by learning, others learn from you, that's fine. Do not allow your vanity to get in the way. It does feel good to have victorious moments when a wrong is righted. It does feel bad to feel from your point of judgment that a right has been wronged.

The human dance, again, we will repeat, is like standing over a prairie watching the wind come down moving the flowers or the wheat in unison. That is like the wave of human consciousness. Today's hero is tomorrow's villain. You see it even in your own news. Teachers of truth, how they came in with their humanness, their spunk of spirit, (Kennedy, Martin Luther King) their inspiration, were turned into paper tigers and destroyed because the wave of humanity is not inspired by truth. It is inspired to see the murkier side of any individual. And what individual does not have a murkier side, whether it is true or false. So a falsehood is presented as truth and truth is presented as a falsehood.

And it is more difficult than ever before to stand in your truth. I ask you to understand that this springtime and the summer coming up you will be forced to make a decision about standing in your truth. Remember what I said. Focus in on that and the world of healing will regenerate you time and time again.

We're going to leave. Through Divine Light, Divine Love and Divine Wisdom and so it is.

Cleansing Your Emotions

Michael: May 3, 1994

In Divine Light, Divine Love and in Divine Wisdom we give thanks for this evening.

In the first place I want to let you know that you as beings of the Earth, as students of truth and in being at one with nature, you have so much to be grateful for. Planetary energies and the healings that you have been feeling are nothing compared to the energies that you will be feeling. It is imperative that you make a decision every day in how you are going to handle your energies. The thing I can tell you is this: You have the opportunity to decide every single moment whether you are going to feel good or whether you're going to feel down. You know the parameters and boundaries of sorrow. You know the parameters and boundaries of anger. And you know the parameters and limitless boundaries of joy.

Through the Earth changes and all the different things that you are going to be feeling, it is important that when you are feeling down that you accept that feeling but to also ask yourself, "Do I really need to go through this feeling again? I know what it feels like. I know how it makes me feel. "And" I know how it affects my body." You need to understand this from a very deep level. When you are very down or very angry, a wave of energy is created through your body upsetting and not only changing your DNA but also releasing chemicals from within that DNA that create body disease and aliments. This is where the disease processes come from.

Think of the release of the chemicals in the following terms. If you have a beaker filled with drinkable water and you add to it acid you will have acidic water. You then add to the beaker an alkaline solution which neutralizes the acid and you again have drinkable water. But that water still has the acidic and alkaline properties. This is what you do to your physical body moment by moment. This pure vessel that comes complete with all of the healing capabilities but has your energies that are constantly adding the acid or the alkaline. Think of it in those terms. When you are angry your body is tense. It is an emotion that fills your body with acid. When you are sad and sorrowful your body is filled with sadness and sorrow.

Now we are not saying to ignore your emotions. But what we are saying is when you experience your emotions ask yourself, "How much longer must I allow myself to feel bad about who I am?" We are not talking about the healing of grieving. We are not talking about the healing of loss. We are talking about the everyday ups and downs.

As you tap into different aspects of yourself that need to be healed, be very cautious that you do not stay in these energies. With the intensity of the Earth changes today and the volatile energies that are in the atmosphere, this constant feeling of being sorry for one's self or feeling a situation to be troublesome again, it is necessary to let them go. Say, "Okay, I need to put my shield up and allow the situation to do its own dance. I am more concerned about my own personal spiritual growth ascending and transcending the physical boundaries and moving beyond the normal personality self and connecting with the God self so that I may be at one beyond these illusions."

It is extremely important that you understand what you are doing to your body. The body is meant to go through a myriad of experiences but when those experiences are stored it is extremely important to get them out, to release them and let them go. The cleansing process is incredibly important right now. Without the cleansing you will feel a collapsing. Without the cleansing there will be a collapsing.

You need to let yourselves know that as spiritual beings in a physical body you experience the human situation very differently than individuals who are not working on themselves consciously. You are much more sensitive and attuned to the actions of other people. You are much more attuned to the emotional impact it has upon your being. You are more attuned to the karmic retribution, the karmic makeup, the repercussions of having to do it over again. And because you are aware of all these things, sometimes you stay too focused in on problems. You stay too focused in on things that you need to learn to release and let go of by the fact that you can observe with your eyes, your third eye, your third ear and your inner voice. They tell you that it is time to move forward.

However, the human says, "I need to straighten this out. I need to change the way humanity sees this situation." You need to let go of that concept and embrace the concept that you need to see yourself as God! These are very powerful times. These are times when Masters walk the Earth. These are times when teachers come in many forms.

So it is really important that during a healing that you think of yourself as a load of chemicals. And you are either going to the toxic chemical spill in your life or you are going to make your life a beautiful sanctuary. If you have to make little noises when you're feeling down and you're spending a lot of time on the feeling then think of yourself as a tanker going through the water. See the tanker getting lighter and lighter as it spills out all the chemicals into the beautiful bay of consciousness. See how hard it is to clean up these spills.

It is really important that you not only see above and below but also on the inside. See where these emotions go. They reach the shores of your body and if they dash up upon the shoreline then they pound upon the shore. Just as a violent storm erodes the shoreline your emotions erode at your health. So it is really important mentally, physically, psychologically, spiritually and esoterically that you as beings understand the integrated process, the true process of integration of the self.

Are there questions about what I have said?

Q. Can you clarify cleansing?

A. Yes. Cleansing in the human sense is a difficult process. It's almost as if you have to remove your consciousness from being human and ask your consciousness to rise up, like the geese that are flying overhead, into a higher state of beingness. And ask that you, in a higher meditative state, bring forth higher and more pure energies that are only in alignment with God to come into your life to pour out the darkness and the heaviness that is within you. One of the techniques that you might want to try using is what the Channel showed you this evening: The balls of light that are from your angels that are being thrown at you breaking up deposits of frozen energy, deposits of negative energy. Cleansing is literally a washing away of the heaviness. What happens when you really get stuck on something, say you get stuck on your parents. It creates first a blocking of your energy from flowing freely through your physical being and starts a cutting off of the energy that supports your health and your vitality. So this is why you forgive. You release and let go because when you dwell on people who have done things against you, you only hurt yourself in the long run. So the cleansing and the releasing is coming from a very high state of beingness that transcends the physical plane and connects you with your higher state of beingness bringing that energy in, almost as if it were an invisible process.

What happens with the human being's consciousness is that it always wants to know why. "How come I can't fix it? How come it's like this? What did I do to deserve? Why aren't they helping me?" And it's always this why and why and why. In human consciousness, the hardest part for human beings is acceptance just because it is!

Your parents have said to you since you were a child, "Just because!" It is! God is! It is! This is the way it is! This is human nature! Why? Because it's human nature! This is the nature you're trying to transcend and the more "whys" you ask the more you stay attuned to human nature. The more you say, "I release and let God handle this" the more you're attuning yourself to the spiritual nature of things.

So the cleansing process is really forcing yourself to reach up and out. Going through many layers, taking many steps back, pulling back and saying "I am going to transcend and go beyond the human. I am going to try and tap into my Higher Self. So cleansing is really done by having a lot of faith.

Through Divine Light and Divine Love and so it is.

"Montanka"
Seeing the Spirit

Michael: May 12, 1994

This evening what I want to talk about is how to work with the energies as they come into your life and to learn that there are many different aspects of your being on the physical Earth.

The aspects of your being encompass the you in the physical body, the you in your imagination, the you in your dream state as you sleep, the you in the meditation state and all the emotional aspects of yourself.

As you are feeling all of the different things that are going on in the external world you are also creating energies in your own internal world. Therefore, it is very important that you understand what your internal world is.

Your external world is the world that exists with or without you. It is the world of individuals, of experiences, of events, of locations and of situations that happen on an ongoing basis. They exist in the world of illusion whether you see them or not.

Many of you who are studying spirituality always see yourself looking outward and perceiving that what you see in the external as real. When the Divine talks about the world of illusion, in truth, what that truly means besides being the shadow aspect of God is that you as individuals do not experience the world as it really is. You experience the world from an inner working. All of your emotional aspects, all of your intellectual aspects, all your senses, all the subtle bodies are the inner workings. Because you are experiencing the external from within, the external is colored by the internal. All of you have experienced a beautiful, bright sunny day but because you're down and out even the beautiful sunny day can't cheer you up. But in essence it doesn't matter what the external world presents you. What matters is the balance of the internal world which you project to the external world that you see.

The thing that you really need to understand is that if you stay locked in your emotional body and stay locked in the intellect, you will never be able to take that quantum leap and move forward and feel the spiritual energies running through you on a continuous basis. You may feel the spiritual energies when you are in meditation. You may feel them when you are calm and life feels good for you.

But how many of you in your joyfulness and your happiness as you are on your path literally stub your toe and all the joy is gone for a moment? This is what happens to all of you on a daily basis. Your spiritual energy is there all the time but because you are constantly stubbing your toe on thoughts or ideas and preconceived notions, the stubbing prevents you from truly enjoying the beauty from within and the God from within so that you can truly see the God in all things.

There is an experiment called "Montanka" which I would like you to try and experiment with. It is the art of becoming invisible and seeing yourself as Spirit. When individuals project their negative concepts and vibrations at you, you can come from the place of Spirit and see yourself as invisible and see their energy just moving through you easily and effortlessly and not affecting you. Try this experiment with your own self. With your own emotions when you are finding yourself in a place where you are saying or thinking: "I can't go on." "I can't take another step forward. The world is just so crazy." "I just don't know what I'm going to do." What you need to tell yourself at at that point is, "Yes, this is a valid emotion, a valid feeling and a valid statement coming from within me, but let me leap beyond that confine that says this is a bad situation." Feel the limitation being created for yourself in making these statements. See the chemical changes you've created from within your body that creates a lack of homeostasis. The buildup of negative energy changes your physiological chemistry which creates anxieties and tensions in your body which you can feel in the pit of your stomach, by a dry throat and a throbbing head. All of these physiological symptoms that occur do so because you in the emotional have set into motion a blocking off of the God force and a blocking off of the healing energies. You have created a cover so that you are no longer bringing light into your body but casting a shadow.

It is important for you as individualized beings to say, "I'm ready to take the next leap." The next step is into Spirit and stop getting stuck in the confines of all of your emotions. It is transcending your emotions and going above, being in the "now" and experiencing Divine Beingness in total. It is the art of being. When you're in the art of being you're beyond your internal world and you are beyond your external world. You just are. You are at one with the God force.

This step into Spirit takes practice. You have to work within the confines of what you know to be true. You have to work within the confines and say, "Okay, this is a bad decision in my life. Now, what do I do? Okay, now I want to take it one step further. I don't want to say that it's a good situation because it is not. Therefore, let me call this a learning situation in my life but for some reason my emotions still get plugged into this and I feel bad. Okay, in order for me to feel bad, it means I had to have experienced it at some other point in my life. Let me go back to my original pain and where this came from so I can start healing it and looking at it and working with it as an aspect of growth as opposed to an aspect that says I must stay stuck. So my new experience tells me when I feel pain it means growth is around the corner." So what we're saying is to take it one step further and say, "Okay, this is an experience and an exercise. There is a portion of me in my humanness that cannot see this as an expression of love. I must learn somehow to raise this energy up higher and know that the pain I am experiencing is growth."

Many people who study the New Age form of metaphysics are told that they create their own pain and that this is a terrible thing. You are never going to get away from pain as long as you are in the human condition. None of the Masters could, so why would you. You are in the human condition. But when you raise your element and your vibration up and go into a humane condition you can temper the pain with experience and knowledge. But you can never eradicate it! This is what the physical body in the physical plane is all about. Limitation. And this is why it is so special when you as individuals can transcend your human limitations and try and push it into the next level and move up into the humane and operate in the physical body as human bringing in spiritual energy. That is a true worker.

That is why Christ said to turn the other cheek. Learn. Grow. Experience. You cannot make anyone angry. Nor can anyone make you angry. No one can make you sad. Nor can you make anyone sad. You make up your own internal world. Your internal world is entirely dictated by your ego, your personality self. And it is very difficult to grow up on the physical plane but with one step at a time, one foot in front of the other you can do it. You can ask for the Master to hold your hand and to take you along this path and help you move forward.

Keep that light, that energy, that love, that consistency. People, it is consistency. Keep the flow of that energy moving through. It's consistency. Bless, pray and think of God twenty four hours a day. In the back of your mind that is all you should be thinking about. You should be dwelling on the indwelling Spirit that gives you life as you sit and breathe and as you feel your physical bodies. So when they say, "Take away my pain." I can no more take away your pain than I can take away your skin.

When people pray, what they are really praying to is to the God force within. And as much energy that is put to that God force within so can the higher force within receive. This is why when you pray in group mind that you are at all different levels of expression of God. But when you pray en mass the energy is so much stronger because all different parts of you can tap into all different parts of the Divine. You are all different aspects of the Divine. You're all different expressions of God.

It is very very important that you understand that your internal world is the only world where you will experience God. And then you will see it in all things on the outside. So this is why I'm saying to you: "Montanka". Walk as if you are invisible. See spirit moving through the world of man, woman, child, the humans. See your body walk through and see your Spirit unaffected by what you see in front of you. See your Spirit only connect with the "Montanka" of the person in front of you, beside you and beyond you.

All of you know someone who is almost impossible to deal with. If that person is so impossible to deal with, imagine how impossible he or she must feel to themselves. Intuitively they know they are not doing the right thing to expedite their growth. They are stuck in a role they don't know how to break out of. Everyone that sees them is in agreement with them because they do not see the Spirit within that person. They see the ego and the personality and they all agree that that person is really difficult. So all of you pray as group mind and say that this person is really difficult. So what happens? The person stays really difficult. And sometimes a person wants to break out of the role that they have been in and they do change. And what happens? People look at this person who has changed and say, "He has really changed...I remember when!"

People are not seeing Spirit in one another. Even in their internal world they hold closed viewpoints of individuals and people. This is why the world does not change. People can't see with the Spirit. They see what the ego says. And then they hold individuals tied down to these images. When you walk as spirit and see the spirit in the person next to you, and you see the Spirit in the person whose impossible (because you acknowledge that God Spirit inside that person) you become their awakener. You may be the only person who can see the Light of the Divine within them. And therefore give them permission to break out of the cage that all humanity has kept them caged in.

You see, you all work as Angels. You all work as teachers. And you are your brother's keeper. You may keep your brother locked inside of you in images, pictures and in ways that may not even be true of who he is today. People who never change and act out a role that they learned do so because they cannot see "Montanka". They cannot see the Spirit within.

It is very important from within that you forgive. Forgive everyone who has hurt you and forgive everyone you have hurt because if you don't forgive you create a bond that's stronger than steel and until you see the Spirit in them, they are bound to you. It just takes one to release the chain, otherwise you will reincarnate with them over and over again.

So it is very important that you understand the difference between the internal world and the external world. The external world is nothing, nothing at all. It's the internal world.

You as individuals who study truth, when you hear your mission and see that you can create change know that it is not good enough to keep it within yourself. You must walk as "Montanka" on the Earth and make changes. You must do something to create change. Every person, no matter what their job is, can contribute something to the change of the Earth and the people around them. From the garbage man, doctor, those in their ivory towers, the multi-millionaire to the person on welfare there is something each and everyone of you can contribute to the world to create infinite change. You must do something. Not just pray on Saturday or Sunday. Not just meditate once a week or once a month but you must do something from within yourself every moment. If you do not, you will come back again and again into the physical form until you wake up and say, "Okay, I've been a child long enough. Now it is time to take care of my family." And that is how you have to think of every single person. Think of each person as a member of your family. You are one big family, group mind, group consciousness and all different aspects of God created in many different forms.

To understand the inner world and the outer world understand the Spirit. Understand your mission and only you know what your mission is. It takes being still. It takes walking as Spirit on the Earth.

We will end for tonight. We give thanks. Through Divine Light and Divine Love and so it is.

Recovery

Michael: May 19, 1994

Tonight I want to talk to you about your life. Your life is in recovery. Everyone is or has been going through the various changes in growth. Your whole life and all of your actions are spent in recovery. Recovering your spirituality. Recovering your love. Recovering your truth. Recovering the Diving Being and the Divine Essence. And with recovery or with bringing back this transformational change in being, you will find that as you move closer and closer to your very center, that all of the discord that you have been holding onto with the mind will gladly release itself.

The only reason you hold onto the discord in the mind is because it has not only become a habit but it has become a place where your fear can reside. What I mean is that where there are aspects of fear in an individual, the fear many times is wrapped up in an issue of anguish, pain or hardship. As you start undoing this hardship and this pain, you find that in the center most core of it is a fear. And what that fear energy is, on many different levels, is the fear of loving the self. It is the fear of just being.

Many people say, "I was in a relationship and just broke up the relationship. Now I cannot stand to be alone." Well, they are not feeling the pain of the broken relationship. They are feeling the fear of getting to know themselves. They are getting into the fear and they are trying to cover their fear of seeing the inner most core of themselves. Individuals who run from relationship to relationship to relationship with no healing time at all in between are masking their pain. They are masking their truth. They are masking their fear. There is such a fear

112

in being alone and knowing who they are that they run to someone else to be their mirror. They are afraid that if they look at the mirror within themselves they will not like what they see and if they cannot like what they see, how can anyone else like them? These are the individuals who never take a moment for reflection of the self.

It is quite ironic that many people connect themselves to the material wealth and the showing of that wealth and good. Now, we are not saying that material objects in themselves are useless. What we are saying is the identification of the self with the material object or person gives a validity and worth on a very superficial level. We are not saying that really wealthy people are superficial or are we saying individuals without a penny are highly Divine. What we are saying is, that on this physical plane, what makes it so difficult for people to recognize who they are is that in their process of recovery they project images of what making it means. And on this physical domain making it means having everything of a material nature.

Now can you balance that in Spirit? Yes! But there are those individuals who feel they don't have to work on themselves because they are beautiful and young. They have property. They have a home. They have a large home. They have a big bank account. They have all the people and all the things that they want in their life. And if you were to ask these people what would happen if I were to take all these things away from you. They would say that it would make them very sad. They would feel lonely. In this process of learning to get back to the self, we are not saying to give up your wealth or to give up your material possessions. What we are saying is to learn to identify with your true self. Learn to move a few steps back and say, "This is not a reflection of who I am. Rather this is just a reflection of what I have been able to acquire in the physical plane. This does not represent my spiritual work. This does not represent the pain it has taken me to get to this place of being. This does not represent all my joys and all my triumphs. All this proves is success and my capability for material objects." They are very temporary for when you die, they do not belong to you.

In the working process as you go through all your self discoveries, discovery of self, family, friends and of the Divine, there is not anyone on the entire planet Earth that really seems to be able to grasp that God is really in charge of all things. There is not one aspect or one incident on this Earth that Divine Beingness is not aware of. There is not one aspect in any individual whose motives are not known by the Divine and whose motives are being motivated by the Divine.

So in this physical plane of Beingness you can actually tap into Spirituality at all times. That Divine State of Beingness is there every single moment. You think it is by coincidence that so many people are becoming awakened. So many people are rediscovering who they are. So many people are trying to run in alignment with the truth. So many people are being turned on to alternative ways of being. This is not a coincidence. This is a universal alarm clock that is going off and each individual is going through their own recovery process just like each individual is going for an operation. They wake up after the operation and they call it the recovery.

So as you go through your processes, as painful as they may be, you need to allow yourselves some time for recovery, and say, "Okay, I just had an operation, I just made a transformational change in myself." And when you are in pain and you are going through something like this, you need to say to yourself, "I just had an operation. I'm going through this consciously. I don't need the anesthesia." And how to release and let go human pain is to say, "Okay God. I'm still trying to make it go my way. Every time I find it go my way I know I'm going to fall flat on my face So how about Divine Beingness? I make a partnership with myself to contact the Divine so that I can raise my consciousness so I don't get hung up on other peoples words or other peoples readings or teachings. When I tap into that inner voice within myself that teaches me my own lesson and I go to my own chapter, and say, "Okay, I've done this before, I've run this pattern before. I know this pain. Why do I know this pain? I know this pain because of X, Y, and Z. Divine Beingness, take me to the summary page where the answers are. Let me see the answers so it will end the way I want it to end."

There is a certain part of human consciousness that has not raised up that innermost aspect that wants someone to say, "You were right!" What happens is this constant inner cheering team going on saying, "Why am I not that spiritual?" "Why am I not living in that area?" or " How do they know that stuff and not me?" You have so many different thoughts in your head and that is the game of life. Sometimes you are up at bat and you hit a home run. Sometimes you are the winning team and sometimes you are your own losing team. Sometimes the audience is cheering you on and sometimes they are flagging you down and sometimes they are not even paying attention.

So there are all these different aspects of yourself going on all at the same time. It is no wonder your spiritual path becomes such a struggle at times. Over here you are worried about the Earth changes. Over here are your bills. Over here how are you going to appear to others. You have all these mish-mash thoughts going on. So can you imagine to try and stay in focus on God to try and stay in alignment with your higher self? No wonder it gets so confusing. Do you have the time to meditate and to do your affirmations?

You can connect with God in all things. The God presence is in the fabric of everything in your life. Finite words describe nothing. My words cannot describe the intensity and the purity of Being. And all other words fall by the wayside. Life changes or does not change because without an evolutionary understanding of the God process from within, the Earth changes within themselves will just be a process which humanity as a mobile consciousness must go through. So when I say that you are in recovery, get with the sources and with all of the words that recovery actually means. Put yourself in a state of wonderment and discovery and every moment when that higher energy comes through as it swishes through, you will feel all of your energies come up and percolate and you will truly feel that you are in a state of inheritance. So it is not a good time to hold on to old things. It is time to weed out the emotional closet, the mental closet, the physic closet and give it to the salvation army of God. Okay, get rid of it! Say, "Okay Michael, pull up the truck and put this stuff inside it." The next time you see the Salvation Army, visualize yourself putting all your stuff in the bag and release the bag.

I will end now. Through Divine Love, Divine Light and Divine Wisdom and so it is.

Lessons on Being Spiritual
in the Human Plane

Michael: June 2, 1994

In the first place, I want to thank you for allowing yourselves to take this moment and opportunity to come into this area. We are going to continue to learn about being spiritual and working with that spiritual energy in the human plane.

For most of you, the mundane world, the world that you live in, creates such turmoil and has such tension and has so many things happening that you find it very difficult to maintain your focus when all these energies are knocking you around. You may start off the day with the highest of intentions. You do your affirmations, center and focus yourself and say, "Today is the day that people do not take me off my center."

But then what happens? A person calls you up and comes into your space. They have an image of who you are and you buy into that image. You therefore have to respond in the way that fits the image they see you to be. Or you walk into a situation saying, "No, today I'm going to work on releasing and letting go. I'm going to forgive all these different vibrations that are around me because I really need to create a clearing for myself. I need to grow. I need to become more at peace with myself." And then again, you walk into a different group of people and because of their back biting or gossiping or their other negative energies, you get sucked into the feeling that you need to push them away. Now your focus is in on protecting yourself against the

117

negative comments of the people. You are sitting there, the best that you can saying, "Okay, I'm going to let this go." And then another person comes into your face and you say, "You know what, I can't stand those people, I wish they would just leave me alone." And there you go. You are off your path. You are sitting on a log. You are not making movement anymore because you have allowed all these other interferences to get in your way.

In being human in the physical form, maintaining that spiritual level of enlightenment is very difficult. It is very difficult to stay in a very warm, peace-filled, loving state because you have all these different outside intrusions. It is a moment by moment experience.

We are trying to express to you to the best of our capacity to spend as much time as you can working on yourself, releasing and forgiving situations within yourself. Now I'm not saying that you are all negative beings filled with so many things that you have to work on forgiveness twenty four hours a day. What I'm talking about in forgiveness is that releasing and letting go. Releasing the energy behind the situation.

You are going to encounter individuals everyday that are filled with anger. That is who they are. That is their truth. You are going to meet individuals everyday that are filled with a sense of peace. That is their truth. You are going to meet individuals everyday that are in a state of confusion, a state of alarm, a state of emergency. You are going to meet individuals everyday that enjoy trauma so much they don't know how to get out of it. And you are also going to meet people everyday who are working on themselves and you need to ask yourself out of all those different types of people that you run into, which person do you identify with the most.

As you are going through the different roles that individuals play in their human life, do you get the most charge when your life is filled with drama? For some of you, it's very difficult to get out of that pool of drama. It's just become so much a part of your life. It's almost in your blood. It becomes a part of your bloodstream.

What we're trying to say is that when you work on forgiveness, it is releasing. It is like sending down to yourself a rope, or a ladder so that you are able to climb out of this pool of consciousness. Because that is all it is. It is a pool of consciousness.

You have to understand that what you choose to do as a personality self on a daily basis to maintain your substance, working for a living, is the role you chose for yourself so that you can work out your karma.

Most of you in this room have had such intense karmic backgrounds that the job placements that you are in now are really about balance, about balancing out your power. You are all in positions of power. It is all about your own personal power and your personal struggles.

What happens? Because all of you are open, you become like a television screen or a movie screen. People project their stuff on your screen. So what do you do? You reflect back what they are giving you. And this is what happens with most people who are open spiritually or psychically. People project. You reflect, like a screen. You're like a big drive-in movie theater. All these people come in and they park themselves in front of you and you are not really listening to yourself. You are listening to the response that they are giving you. You are listening to what they think about you as opposed to what you think about yourself.

The more and more that you work on yourself, the less and less their chatter becomes important. And the more and more you stop becoming the television or the movie screen and the more you start emanating and radiating who you are. And you become impervious to their comments. You become impervious, you become invincible against their statements and you learn to hear with a different ear. You learn not to hear, "Ugh, listen to what they have to say, look how they are treating me today." But rather you listen differently and say, "That person must be in a lot of pain. Do you ever hear how they are so sarcastic all the time? That person must have gone through so much stuff, that they're afraid to be real. All they can do is talk about how wonderful, talk about how great, how superior they are and how little everyone else is." And when you really start listening with a different ear, listening with that third ear, you really start listening. You start seeing that there is so much pain in the human condition and human dilemma. Individuals are constantly barraging one another with their pain. But it comes out in the source of hurtful comments and hurtful actions. People who go out and purposely hurt others are hurting the most themselves. They are the ones who have created the biggest void between themselves and their Divine. The Divine is still within them. They just are not able to tap in to it.

All of you all do it to yourselves in different areas of your life. Where you're having a lot of pain about relationships is where you create the biggest barrier between you and the relationships. So you find yourself associating with other individuals who also cannot get into relationships. If you associated with people who are happy about themselves and happy in their relationships, you would be absorbing their energy of love because the energy and vibration they have surrounding themselves is filled with balance and the understanding of the laws of prosperity. Like attracts like. It doesn't mean that you're going to take their partner away from them. What it means is that you are immersing yourself in this energy and vibration filled with love. Therefore, this vibration becomes so powerful within you that the radiating factor goes out and a partnership comes to you.

Now we're not suggesting that those of you who are single in this room never see each other again. What we are saying is to think about how you perceive yourself. Do you see yourself as an individual? Do you see only the external aspect of the physical human body? Do you only see the embodiment of the clothing, of the face, of the skin, of the hair? Do you only see yourself as far as flesh, blood and muscle? For most of you, this is true. This is how you see yourselves. You say with one mouth, "No, I see the inner beauty in all people." and you say with the other mouth, "Oh my God, that's what I look like in a bathing suit?" So, there are two mouths speaking at the same time here.

Now we are not saying to not take care of your body. What we are saying is first take care of your spiritual body. Acknowledge that spiritual body and say, "Look, that spiritual body is that body which really emanates and radiates the most powerful, wonderful, vibrant aspects of myself. It radiates love, it has this attracting factor. If I am truly one with the Universe, if I'm part of the Divine Energy, then my Divine partner is out there somewhere, in the physical form for me. If that's what I truly want this lifetime, I'm going to put it out there that the Highest of the High, the Highest of the High comes to me and I am attracted to them like a magnet that is irresistible. There is no way that the magnetizing force between me and that individual can be separated."

121

But see what happens is you don't usually stop at that. You usually go, "and they have to be wealthy, and they should be tall and so on." You attach conditions to what you put out to the Universe.

Most of you do not like diets but you put out, to the Universe, that you want a spiritual diet when it comes to your greater good. Do you understand what we're trying to get at here? In the living of spiritual life, in the fullness of expecting the highest of the high, you assume you're going to get something less when it comes to a partner, a job or any other area of your life. You ask for the highest of the high and then you then attach the conditions. You try to reduce the highest of the high. You go for the spiritual skinniness. Skinniness and spirituality do not go together. Spirituality is about fullness. When you think about your consciousness, think Rubinesque. Think full. Think huge. Think about those beings who stand along the waters of the Nile in Alexandria, those gigantic statues of the pharaohs, of the high priestess and this is where you will get a sense and source of greatness.

When people were really in alignment at one point with spirituality, did they build little thimble sized pyramids? No, they built these huge pyramids. When people think of expansive land, are they talking about a backyard. They're talking about the West and the expansive land mass that's out there. But when you think about yourself and talk about your own spirituality you always separate it. You separate it between your physical wants and needs and what you think you can attain.

You are at your spiritual best at this moment. This is where you revere this God/Goddess energy at your spiritual best right now. Everyday, every moment that you breathe you're being given another opportunity to achieve even greater greatness. So we're going to ask you as Angels, as Guardians, as Teachers, as Masters to step out of the limitations that you have placed yourselves in the human form and join hands with the spiritual greatness that is inside of you. Look in the mirror and don't say disappointedly, "What I see and what I give myself is all of my spiritual good." And LOVE what you see in that mirror.

Many of you go beyond what you see in that mirror and go back into things you did that you felt weren't so good about yourself. "Oh, I handled that romance that way. Why did I misjudge that person. Why didn't I do such and such." And so on. So what you see are your so called failures. We see you burning off your karma! We see you leaping into the fire of purification. Some of you coming out in a lot of pain. But if you can witness to yourself that most of the pain you've been in is the burning off of your karma and you can be witness to that pain saying, "Okay, that was something I did but I'm ready to let it go. And you want to know what, it makes me a greater person because I have a better understanding. I have more understanding that I can relate to someone else's confusion. I can relate to their pain and where they've been."

See what happens in the human plane when you're divided of your spiritual knowledge is that you try to match cards. "I had a baby and went through this much pain." "I had a baby and I went through more pain that that." Well, I had a baby and they had to reconstruct me." You match cards instead of saying and acknowledging within that person, "I understand their pain."

Recently we were talking about grieving and when you lose a parent. How that feels when you lose somebody you love and the importance of being there for the other person. The importance of just that simple holding of the persons hand or the acknowledgment. Just the nod of the head and not empty words and being able to be present for that person. It is the same thing when another individual is communicating to you.

So what are we saying to you now? Are we saying when people come out with these really nasty comments to just let them fly past you? For the most part your retaliation is not going to change or alter that individual. What you can do is make yourself a body of glass and feel those comments just moving through you. Surround yourself in a tremendous amount of love and let yourself know that this individual is nothing to you and in the long run the more you let these individuals go, the least likely you're going to meet them in another lifetime. Because guess what? Most of the people you can't stand now you have brought with you! And it's you that brings them. The more you study metaphysics, (think about this, this is the beauty of spirituality) the more powerful you are, the more capable you are of releasing and letting go. The stronger your anger is towards a person the more you bring them to you. They're usually weaker than you are. They're willing to let you go but you're not. You're like an Atlas when you study metaphysics and spirituality. You have strength. So you think to yourself, "Oh wow, why did I bring that person?" Well you have to ask yourself, not why did you bring them but are you willing to let them go? Are you willing to just cut them off, let them go, let them be themselves. They're never going to be anything different than what you see today. You have an earthly saying that leopards don't change their spots. So that also means that you have never changed as individual either in search of truth and spirituality. The only thing that continues to changes in your awareness.

Many of you are going out there looking to be healers. All of you are healers internally and the part of being spiritual in the physical plane is learning how to heal yourself first. And healing yourself in mind, body and spirit. Learning to work with yourself emotionally and spiritually and learning to work with yourself in the physical body. If you can't change your physical form you must learn to bless it, love it and treat it as good as you can. For some people in the physical plane in this lifetime, this is as good as it gets. This is your body and many times what we hear on the spiritual levels are people who are working on themselves so intensely spiritually, but their darkside or the side that holds them back is the side that has them being hung up about the physical form.

The physical form never prevented Buddha from enlightenment. Physical form never stopped any of the female masters from enlightenment. Love knows no physical form. There is no perfect form for Divine Love. The reason we're emphasizing this this evening is that there is not that much time left in the physical plane for all of you to be so hung up on physical beingness. You do what you can do. You bless your food. Make sure you bless your food. You bless your bodies. Bless the people around you as best as you can.

But remember something and again I will always end all these lessons about the same way because I want to remind you every moment that every word out of your mouth is a prayer. Please understand that your babble is heard through the ethers creating and destroying like Shiva. You're always tearing yourself up or building yourself up. And since you are God/Goddess energy Divine, and since one of the golden rules is not to take the name of the Lord in vain and since you are also the Lord, do not take your own name in vain. If the fools that walk in human form around you choose to defame, ask yourself consciously, "I am trying to attract the highest and best for myself? Is it worth the one second of pleasure of slashing an individual to pieces? Is that worth it? Is it worth destroying another persons personality by throwing them in the fire, putting gasoline on their fire and watching them burn?"

I'm not talking about injustice. When you see an injustice being done that is part of your job as a soldier or a spiritual teacher or leader to look at it and to straighten out that injustice. But the highest way you can change that injustice is by constantly revealing the truth. By blessing, keeping your facts straight and being unswervingly true to the truth that motivates you within. Name calling and back stabbing though it may win you points in court, in the physical form it will only create attraction for that individual again in the future in your life. So be very careful how you perceive in all the different arenas in you life, especially legally.

I know I've gone around and around so you may have questions. Why don't you ask them.

Q. Should we still avoid New York City?

A. What you have to understand is that one of the reasons I've been voicing so much concern about New York is that there is going to be much violence in New York and also the continuation and the fluctuation of the various disease patterns that are moving through New York. Besides the vibrational changes that are happening, it is a very dangerous place to walk through.

The vibrational energy in New York City is in a way like the black hole theory. The energy of an exploded star. What has happened is that New York City was a Mecca at one time for higher cultivation and it was a Mecca for learning as well as the creative arts. Over the past 40 years spiraling energy has come into New York City and what it has done is it has slowly eroded that spiritual base. The spiritual vibration is still around New York City, however, it is moving in a counter clockwise pattern creating this vortex of energy that keeps working on the human or the group consciousness of Manhattan as fear. The group consciousness of Manhattan is hatred. The group consciousness of Manhattan at this particular time is about anxiety and emotional distress.

So what we're talking about is that you're literally allowing yourself to walk into a really great emotional storm. Do you understand? So when you as a person walk into New York, you become very drained at the end of the day. It is very important that you do symbolic rituals like showering and cleaning of your aura and this is true for most of the major cities in the United States today. Most of the major cities in the United States have a very very strong energy. The energy has to get a lot stronger before it breaks.

There's going to be a lot of tension. We've talked about the racial wars that are going to happen. It's this energy, the separation between the races right now. And what happens is that humanity starts fragmenting. It starts seeing itself as

127

separate as opposed to whole. And in New York City there is that fragmentation of energy. Now what is happening is these cataclysmic things will start to happen in New York and various other cities, due one group, whether it be race or creed, thinking it is better than the other group. What is happening is these groups are being confronted by their pain. Confronted by their challenges and their truth. They're challenging group mind consciousness. What everyone has forgotten is they've taken three steps back and instead of working towards nature and spirituality and God consciousness, they are working more and more towards a so-called political correctness They have forgotten that the Divine Being is the natural order of things.

It takes all of humanity, like beads on one string, to be raised to higher truth and consciousness. Each aspect from the beginning of man in the form of the black man to the latest evolution of the Caucasian. All of these different vibrations from the yellow man to the brown man to the red man, if they would all sit there and hold their pearls of wisdom and all brought these jewels out and corrected them, knowledge and truth would flow through this planet like never before.

But what is taking place is because so many mis-truths are happening, so many people are seeing this as an opportunity to create a power structure, playing king of the mountain. But the cities themselves are going to fall under their weightiness of their pain and anger. Out of the ashes will rise up a change. But at what cost?

So these are the reasons we are telling you at this moment, that vibrations in major cities are very very hard. If you as a personality self can step through the city without evoking fear, anger and negativity and remember those concepts, those precepts, the precepts of truth and remember that each individual has something great to offer from the beginning of time, then you can walk with your head high through New York. But once you open yourself up you will feel the draining energy and go home in a very tired and exhausted state.

Q. Could you comment on how to get through the food addiction temptation?

A. Well, You are going to have to consciously ask yourself, "Is it worth the feelings of guilt that I project upon myself after the immediate rush? See, it goes so much deeper. There are many other issues attached to this and this is a lengthy answer but we will try and make it brief.

That neediness, whether it's food, sex or alcohol, that emptiness that has started in the beginning part of your life, that aspect within yourself where you go to prove over and over again, "I am not perfection." "I am not love." "I am not worthy." "I am a little poop." "I am not as good as I project myself to be." "I am a hypocrite." "I am a lowly creature." All those vibrations, words, thought patterns, tapes, it's your self-sabotage. It's you knowing where your trap is and setting it up for yourself so that you can fall down with the dirt on your face having everybody in your mind looking down at you going ha-ha, you did it again. It is by agreement in your psyche that you have asked that portion of your psyche to stay in denial, to stay in darkness, to stay as a mute, to not communicate with you about the food that is in front of you. The thing that you can do for yourself is to really, every time you see this, whether the little voice goes off or not, and you're saying it doesn't, is you need to be able to sit there and look and just remember.

See, that's your aspect of denial. It's not that the little voice doesn't go off, it does. It's just that you're in such denial that even though it exists, it doesn't come up. So allowing yourself to sit there and say, "Okay, this is really something I do want. Now can I have it and enjoy it or will I have this and will it really wreck havoc on me? That's the difference between moderation and excess. You can eat sugar in different things in moderation. But what happens is excess comes into your being because you really need to let yourself know you're not as good as you think you are. This is that neediness from you to prove to yourself that you're not as good.

And the thing is, you have so many things you're working on right now. And even though you say you've worked on it, you're working on losing your loved one, changing your status as being a parent, your job, not being in a relationship, friendships and finances. You're working on all these things.

So on another level you're telling yourself, but don't I deserve a treat? Don't I deserve to be good to myself? And the answer you always come up with is <u>no</u>! I'll be more than good to myself. I'll go into excess. So somewhere in that big question of yours, is a lot going on. It's not as simple as not hearing the voice. You have a whole Ferris wheel of little grieves and big grieves, of loss and big losses that you're working through. And even though the Ferris wheel is fun at first, after a while it can be really scary when you can't get off. And the only thing that gets you off of that Ferris wheel for a little while is that sugar, is the food, and the other things.

So somehow you're going to have to allow yourself to have the food but say, "Okay if I do this, what I'm going to do immediately after is go for a walk, or I am going to schedule myself to say that was good as opposed to giving myself this whole big lecture on why I'm bad." This is why we're saying some peoples' bodies are as they are. You have to bless the body as it is. Now we're not saying to use alcohol for medicinal purposes to cover your pain. And we're not saying to use food as medicinal purposes to cover your pain. But if you look at the intensity of what food would do versus alcohol, or what gambling would do versus sexual addiction, even though they're all different kinds of addictions, as long as you're not bingeing and purging and you are keeping your food somewhat in check, you're not really going out on a limb and creating havoc in the world. The only place you are creating havoc is within yourself. And as we said, <u>"Bless your food and in the blessing of your food before you eat it, ask that God give you restraint."</u>

These are very simplistic things and it's much deeper and longer and involved than that but that's the simplest answer I can give you.

What we are going to do is to end. Through Divine Love, Peace and Happiness, enjoy yourselves, align yourselves and try and remember what we said this evening. And so it is.

Acceptance of Another
and Love
Michael: June 9, 1994

We ask that a circle of light and protection form in this room creating an arena of truth, peace and harmonious action between the beings that are here in physical form and the beings that enter the room in spirit. We ask that Jesus Christ stand in the center of the room acting as the Light of Lights as the angels sing and dance around the room to bring in the Truth this evening.

In the first place, we want to give thanks for all of you who are here. We will continue to look at the lessons on what it is to be human in the physical plane and to work with your spirituality.

Tonight, I really need to talk to you about love. But before we get into the focused arena of love, we need you to take a look at how you as individualized beings of self conduct yourself on a daily level.

Many times at work, at home, at play you will find individuals whose main crux of being is making fun of other people or their situations. They stand there. They belittle people. They see someone and they are always good for the sarcastic comment or the nasty remark. And it goes on from there to people escalating to a true character assassination at the cost of surrounding the individual with feelings of being unwelcome and feelings of pain. Why do individuals do this in the physical plane to one another? Usually the one doing the name calling is an individual who has no sense of self and is so afraid that the weakness within them will show. So what they do first is attack an individual. That individual, therefore stands there getting ready to attack back. As the individual is defending his or her honor, they don't see beyond their attacker's mask which shows that within that person is an individualized being with a tremendous amount of pain and suffering, a sense of unworthiness and a sense of being unlovable.

The reason that we are saying this to you is that each and everyone of you in your daily lives run across individuals who push your buttons and it is important for you to understand why these people act as they do. Most of them are acting at a sense of no power and a wanting to empower themselves. In the past these people were called bullies. In this day they are called leaders. What these bullies try to do is to evoke a primal fear. A fear evoked from the point that if you like someone just for who they are and get to know them just for who they are, then you are stepping outside of the confines of this group-packed consciousness. Remember, mankind is group consciousness. If you really step outside the pack and really get time to investigate another person, you might find that there are so many things in common that you might actually like the person that you have been standing there making fun of.

But will you like that person with the whole group making fun of you? See, human beingness, on certain levels, is very immature. It will only like others if the one kingpin says, "Yes, I like them too." And the sway of energy moves and everyone opens up their arms and that person gets welcomed into the swell.

That happens in religion, politics and families. Like a misguided mobile. You have seen mobiles. You press one and they all move. All scattered. And that is what happens with that human energy. Human energy, even though psychologists call it a dysfunction, is the way humanity functions. But all of humanity has this sort of dysfunction within itself in the human consciousness, the group mind.

So when Divine Consciousness comes to Earth and speaks of love, speaks of opening up and accepting yourself and others for who they are, it is looked upon as a sign of weakness. Christ was killed for speaking love and truth. Krishna was attacked for speaking love and truth. The Dalai Lama was thrown out of his own country for speaking love and truth. Tibetans today are tortured for holding the banner of God high. So what is it with the human plane of consciousness in its relentless search of wanting to know who it is and wanting to feel a purpose, an embracing love and at oneness? A feeling of belonging? To have someone love them? Or to love someone else? What is it in human beingness that the very thing they desire is the very thing they trample under their feet? They stay with their steely knives. They take their fences and rip it into the Earth. They take humanity and pin one against the other. So what is it in humanity at one hand that they look for spirituality and truth yet with the other hand they actually seek and crave power and destruction?

At this point humanity has to come to its own inner conclusion. The conclusion is that if you see me for who I really am you will not like me. I will become unlovable and without love I cannot exist. So what I will do in order to forfeit love is I will just accept people liking me at the cost of shooting down my brother or my sister or all my relations on the Earth. The animals. The trees. The water. The earth itself.

Humanity is to frightened at this point in its developmental beingness to open up the next step and say Divine Love and Divine Truth is the motivating factor that keeps my breath alive. It is Divine

Love and Divine Truth that allows me and propels me and gives me the energy to speak as a mealy mouth being saying nothing but negative things about my fellow human beings.

There is such fear on a deep rooted core of humanity that if it faces its ugly truth, that Divine Beingness will reject it. So what it does in defense of itself is to quickly reject Divine Beingness thinking that Divine Beingness is going to play by the same rules that humankind does. That Divine Beingness will fight back trying to defend itself against the negative energy. When in reality and in truth, Divine Love and Divine Beingness just is. Love is and permeates, going way beyond the confines of human beingness. Divine Love and Divine Truth does not even entertain the little goings on of human beings. And this is why within the laws of karma on this physical plane when it reaches a pinnacle it will have to come to a balance. It is not God who punishes human beingness. It is not the Divine who comes down with a sword to slice humanity in half. But is rather the consciousness of human beingness under the weight of its own intense fear, anger and suffering that will crush itself like a star imploding upon itself and everything being sucked in it like the black hole.

It is one thing to have pride in the fact that Divine Beingness created you as a unique being in your own gender, in your own race, in your own religion. It is one thing to say, "Thank you God for this Divine gift, for this experience and for who I am as a being on this physical plane." And it's another thing to say, "I am the only one." You are not the only one. Not any of you.

You all suffer at some points of your life as individuals who are intolerable of others. You find yourself saying, " How do I handle this person? I can't take it anymore." And you ask, "Should I take this?"

And we say, No, you do not have to take unkindness. You do not have to stand for meanness. We said before you must stand firm in your truth and be able to meet with the enemy. And then in the end you forgive. You let go. You release and you bless that person. You let them go. You give them what they gave to you. You do not take their stuff into your heart. You do not take their anger into your soul. You confront them and say, "Excuse me, excuse me. I do not remember inviting you into my life to hurt me. Take your painful weapons and go play with someone else who wants to entertain that game." For the most part they will be embarrassed. They will deny that they even know what you are talking about or it will anger them even more. And if it angers them more, you tell them again, "I did not invite you into my life. You have invited yourself and in my life, which is sacred. I invite my friends and I excuse my enemies, therefore I excuse you."

It is important that you call a spade a spade. It is important that you call the being for who they are. For if you quiver in niceness, "Oh, I can't say that, I have to be nice," then you are not working on God's terms. If you go back and you look within the Christ as he walked on the Earth you will see that he threw the change makers out of the temple. Those beings who confront you. They are the change makers coming into the Divine Father's house. Your body, your mind, your consciousness is a temple. And until each and every one of you reclaim your rightful place as the priest and high priestess walking on the Earth, the living, loving, representation of God, the return of the Christ Consciousness within each and every individual, and work with that fervor, and that firmness and blessing yourself and releasing and letting go understand that as the crucifixion occurred, it will happen in your own life through your own pain, your own suffering and the challenges you go through. You do not need anyone in your life asking the crowd, "Should we put this person on the cross?" You do that every time you allow someone to make you feel bad. Do you understand what we are saying? You allow them!

"Oh, but you don't know what they did to me," you say. But you don't know that you have opened up your heart and entrusted yourself to beings that you knew deep down inside could not be trusted. You did not have the emotional fortitude and therefore allowed yourself to be hurt by someone. You can only be hurt if you are giving love on condition. How about that? When you give unconditional love you can never be hurt. If you as an adult allow another adult to hurt you, then you allowed it to happen because it was love on condition.

You will eventually get to the place where peoples' barbs and their comments will pass through you. They will be empty because you will understand on a deeper level that they are coming from a severe point of pain, jealousy and anguish. You have something they can't have, so they are trying to attack you. You may want to tell them that, but they will not hear you.

This evolutionary process of being human and understanding the principals of love is very difficult for you as beings of truth because you are also beings who live in the illusion. So on one level you have one hand on God and one hand on the illusion so it is very hard to see the truth at times. Even though you know the sun is out there when it is a foggy day, it sure doesn't feel like the sun is out there. Even though logic says you would not be able to see your hand in front of your face if the sun wasn't out there. This is what's so funny about humanity. It is sunny but there just happens to be clouds in front of the sun. "Oh, it's raining out, there's no sun today." That is the most bizarre statement human beings can make. But you do the same thing. You say, "I'm in so much pain. Where's God?" Don't you do the same thing? As above, so below, and most of you are staying in the below. Okay, so it is time you get to the above and climb out of the below, or even get to the middle. And the next time it is raining out, please catch yourself. Say, "Gee it's raining, it's bright out there but it's raining."

Remember that love is the most important healing aspect of your life. There are those who have lost or are losing a loved one. They are leaving or have left the physical plane and it is difficult for you as human beings to know that the physical touch is gone or will be gone soon. So it is an extremely important experience in being human, in being physical, to mourn and grieve. That is also your sign of love, that is your releasing and letting go. Your love and the love of the other people you recruit into this situation will help their soul make their transition very smooth.

It is at that point, my dear ones that you really do need the support of the people around you understanding what love is. This is why tonight we speak of love. Love is the only healing agent that is going to help you move through this experience. It is going to help you tremendously to move through the pain of human suffering that you are experiencing now and will continue to experience. If you open yourselves up to love and you open yourselves up to the love that is there from Divine Spirit and the other people who love you in your life, then they will be your float, cradling you and embracing you while you go through this sea of change.

While you personally go through this sea of transformation, it is very important that you understand that this message of love is also something that you need to hear because people will be saying mean things about people with different disease processes. And you need to stand with courage, not to fight them, not to battle with them but to let them know that you are talking about a real person.

Allow yourselves to just take a moment and feel the loving arms of truth and love surround you, embrace you and hold you. Love is a powerful healer and we promise that we will not leave you.

We are going to end. Through Divine Love, Divine Light and Divine Wisdom and so it is.

Truth/God Realization
Michael: June 16, 1994

Sananda:

We give thanks to you for being here. I come here this evening as Sananda to speak to you before our brother Michael does. This evening you have called upon my presence to work with the other workers of Light and this I can tell you: Your prayers have not only been heard but they have been answered.

I ask that when you go deep into your heart, especially during these moments on the Earth plane, that you don't speak in flowery adjectives about yourself. It is a time for pulling back the veil and to stand naked before the Son of God and say, "This in my truth." And as the Son of God and the Light of Divine Truth shines upon your eternal being, the shadow cast from the darkness within your being whether it is long or short is not a reflection of who you are but rather a reflection of the light that you pass back to the Divine.

In being human you are going to have shortcomings. In being physical it is always going to be an upwards struggle to stay in alignment with Spirit. And this I say to you this evening and never let it sleep within your heart or fall deaf within your ears. May you hear this. May you know this and may you feel this. <u>Your truth never dies!</u> <u>Your lies never die!</u> So always ask yourself, "Will I be in truth or will I be in a lie?"

You were all talking over the weekend about light and dark and I ask that all of you to check moment by moment your truth and your spiritual nature. Not one of you here can tell me that you don't know when you're not doing the right thing. You cannot tell me you forgot

141

because all of you know. It is only by convenience that you do not act. Does that sound too heavy for your ears to hear? Too hard for your emotions to face? Too much for your intellect to accept? I say this with conviction and honesty and with the approval of God.

How is it that you can recognize it later? Granted, some of you are still like small children too afraid to speak the truth which will ensure that words do not come out the wrong way. But that fear does not stop you from trying. "Think before you act" is extremely important. If you think you are going to sound like a fool, then do not speak. In your heart of hearts you know you are being foolish. And in your heart of hearts you know it is your ego asking for compliments when you say, "Do I sound like a fool?" When you feel that you sound like you are wise, at that point you are a fool because wisdom does not need any such feeling.

I will leave now. Michael needs to come through this channel this evening but I will be coming more and more until you feel that awakening within your heart and in your soul.

I will say this once. So many foolish people ask if darkness, Lucifer, Satan, the devil exist. In your world, yes. And pity the fool who says, "Just don't buy into it!" because they become a tool for the darkside. That's what the darkside would like you to think. That someone is trying to get over and they want you to believe that they are not. You will learn different ways of protecting yourself. But the best way to protect yourself is to speak from the heart. Think before you speak. Do not take this new found sort of truth and go slashing people by the throat. Rather slash the ties that you have created through the centuries by using truth and remember when you use these tools for destruction, only you in the long run can be destroyed. So act as

Vishnu in your life and in your world and also remember that only the Divine is the sustainer.

Michael:

We are going to continue with our lessons in working on yourselves in the physical plane. Here you are in the physical plane. Centuries go by. The rules change ever so slightly. Each generation believes it has re-invented the wheel. Each generation truly believes it has invented human consciousness.

Yes, for this Earth plane and the epic it is going through, more and more beings are becoming aware. Does that change the intensity of accessibility to God? Does that change the power of the Divine Beingness as it has been throughout eternity and will continue to be?

Each generation believes it has re-invented the wheel. And as each group of humanity becomes awakened toward its spiritual enlightenment, it says to itself, "Ah-ha, I can almost go out and touch the moon." In this generation you can get in a little spacecraft of your own and get to the moon. But does that mean that the moon has gotten any closer? No, the moon has always been right there. It is just now that you have a vehicle to get there. And that is the same thing that is happening with this New Age movement. In a lot of ways it is built on ego, on darkness and on black magic. In its puffiness and its egoness it says, " Oh, I'm better than ..." "I'm greater than..." "I'm more than..." "Try this method, you'll get to God quicker." "No, no only this method will get you to God." There is not a quick method to get to God.

You take some flour, some baking soda, a little bit of salt, an egg, some milk and some chocolate and mix these ingredients all together, bake them and you then have brownies. And you think that if you take a little bit of Buddhism, add some metaphysics, study with a teacher, study from many teachers and put all of this together that you become God realized. That is not how it works. Books do not make you God realized. Channeling does not make you God realized. Listening to me does not make you God realized. What makes you God realized is GOD! Get it?

So in studying metaphysics and spirituality understand it is not just about affirming "I am Divine Wisdom." What you are basically trying to do is brainwash yourself. "I am God realized." "I won't pay my taxes this month, but I'm God-realized." "I know I should clean my room but it's more important to go meditate on being God realized." "I know I shouldn't be as mean and nasty to those people in my life but I am God-realized." When I'm in the gym I know I look better than them but I'm waiting to be God-realized." "Don't know when I'm going to die but I'll die more closer to God than you because I am God realized." So what happens is when you start saying these things, the affirmation or the prayer does generate the vibration around you. I do not dis-credit that and neither should you. Prayers are very powerful. They supercharge the environment that you are in. But there is a little axiom that you were all taught by your parents as you grew up. It is, "Actions speak louder than words". So when you go through your Akashic records, guess what you are really going to look at? Your actions!

You may say that you released and let that go. Yes, but while you are releasing and letting go you still continue to do the action. Do you understand what we are trying to get at? To change your behavior as well as changing the way you think. Changing the way you think is one thing, but changing your behavior and forcibly changing yourself to really be a receptacle for Divine Consciousness and enlightenment is hard work. It means suffering. It means pain. It means banging your shins every once in a while. It means confrontational situations with other human beings. How do you know whether or not you have accomplished your goal unless you had that confrontation?

It is really great to say that you have an air conditioner that works, but do you need it in the winter time? No! You want it in the summer. So in the same shape and fashion, it's okay to say you have worked on these issues, but how do you know you are successful until you have walked into the energy and unless that energy confronts you and you are able to deal with it effectively.

When you work on yourself psychologically, what you are doing is you are working at getting some of the mental pieces of the puzzle to cooperate with what you really believe in. Metaphysics and psychology could be blended. That is truly what it is for. It is to mentally put your puzzle together the way that you believe is correct for you. Not what Freud thinks or what other psychologists think about growth but what metaphysical teachers of truth have been teaching for centuries to help individuals align to the highest truth so they understand their actions in order to move forward.

You may have read a story of individuals who go away and study spirituality and suffer and struggle and toil. They may even leave the secular life to live a life of religion and to study with great teachers. They do all the things that they have been taught to become God-realized. And then they hear a story about a person who has murdered an individual and in the killing of that individual, the murderer receives enlightenment because it was the Master that they killed, not physically but figuratively. That act awakened the murderer for whatever reasons the Divine had in mind. And which one of you after all your pain and suffering and struggling and separation and change would be able to handle seeing someone who to you did absolutely nothing but the most horrible act and was rewarded with spiritual God-realization? You don't know that man or woman's history. You don't know that man or woman's background. This is what happens on this physical plane when you are in the here and now in this physical body.

Too many of you ask for a pay-off right now. Many of you will not receive a pay-off right now. You do not know what your future lives will entail, nor do you know what your personal future holds for you. The greatest seer does not know God's plan for the rest of your life. So what you need to do and how you need to work for yourself, if you can allow your consciousness to accept this, is you do it without serving the self. You do everything to serve God without any expectation of reward. Without any expectation of enlightenment. You just love to serve God because you are so grateful that God gave you life and you are alive. So many people forget to give thanks for the very moment that they are alive.

Many of you in this room have experienced the loss of a parent, a friend, a child. That is the alternative. In life there are only two alternatives. Being alive or not being alive. Many of you act as the sleeping or the walking dead in the world, mumbling and groaning and moaning at God about your daily activities on this Earth plane. Think about the alternative when you groan about food shopping: no shopping/no food. Where you live: no home/homelessness and so forth. Think about the alternatives when you groan. Be grateful and praise the Divine Beingness for all that you do have instead of groaning about the lesson or lessons that you may be going through.

After looking at all that you have to be thankful for you still groan and persist to spit in the eye of God by saying, "What have you given me?" then don't turn your head too quickly when you hear someone who you have least expected becomes God-realized. At least they knew they were ungrateful for everything. Maybe they didn't want to live but maybe what they needed was the gift of life. A life that was totally worth living. Why me? Why me? Do you know what that sounds like? So when you want to whine, join the spiritual AA and get in the twelve steps spiritual program and put down the wine glass and pick up the glass of life. Because when you say, "Why me?" you are the anti-Christ AA. Anti-Christ anonymous, okay. You want to know where the anti-Christ is? Look in the mirror folks. You want to know where the Christ is? Look in the mirror folks. Who are you representing?

We are going to end and we give thanks and I give thanks to Sananda. Through Divine Beingness and so it is.

Pain/Compassion/Laughter
Michael: July 14, 1994

I ask that Divine Beingness and Divine Consciousness enter into the room. I ask that Sananda as well as the other teachers and angels who are present in this room creating a circle of light and healing, open the doors to the other beings of Truth to come in and listen.

We give thanks to Divine Beingness and Divine Essence for this moment, this opportunity in time to speak. For the communication of words is the rippling effect which goes into the Universe and shifts and shapes the fabric of the Earth of human consciousness and creates new thoughts, creates healing and creates peace.

Sananda will come in this evening for a short time and then we will continue with the lessons.

Sananda:

All of you have mentioned you have friends and family going through intense pain; changes and upsets and feelings that are creating stagnation in their lives. Some of you know others who are in such fear and pain that they don't know what to do with themselves. They express this pain over and over again. And in the expression of their pain they hope that maybe someone will turn to them and say that they love them, they see them, they hear them. When you see these people in pain, when you see them going through these wild contractions within themselves, you can stand back and allow them to be. You can pray for them. You can verbally give them support even though they many not hear you. And then you have to ask what is this experience like so that you can look at and say I understand.

In watching a woman go through labor; the nine months that she holds on to a child and feels the changes in her body bringing joy and sometimes pain until the final moment when the child must be born.

If you have ever seen anyone have a child or if you have had a child yourself, you recognize when you are writhing in pain, that your consciousness is not focused in on anything but the experience of your physical body.

Even with a support system around you, you don't want anyone touching you or holding you because the pain is so intense. Then there is relief, a moment of pleasure, and then the contractions once again bring more pain. And while this child is being born many things are happening. For some it is the experience of joy in seeing a whole wonderful healthy baby. For some it is the pain of a mother losing a child or having a child being born in a state of deformity. There are a myriad of experiences happening during the process of giving birth to another human.

My dear children, this evening, as the Earth and her changes occur heaving in contractions in the form of thunderstorms and the water breaking in the form of floods and the sweat in the form of these heat waves you find that people all around you are giving birth to their true selves. Some are writhing in pain only to find that they have had lifetimes of never growing and always harboring fear and disdain. And there are those who are working very diligently and hard and are finding that their birth process is painful but the miracle of just making it through these Earth changes, making it through the spiritual birth process is so incredible that they don't care how it comes out, just so long as they come out whole and healed.

So just as you cannot comfort the mother in that time of peak pain, you cannot really comfort people who come to you and are complaining. They cannot hear your answers. They are going through their time of contraction. They are going through their time of labor. This is not to say to have no compassion for your fellow human beings. This is not to say not to go out and feed the poor or look for shelter for those who have no homes. This is not to say to not take care of the infirm. What I am saying is not to get wrapped up in someone else's pain that you forget to stand witness to the birthing of those around you who are in true celebration of the process of new life. You need to learn the laws of compassion. This is something Michael has told you over and over.

You are in witness to the new cycle of humanity and its fledgling state. You must look around yourself everyday at the creation as it is today. This is the peak of humanities intellect. It is the peak of humanities spirituality.

I hear many of you complain about where you live. I hear you complain of what you don't have. I have not heard you bless all the things that are good in you life. Remember now more so than ever before that every single word creates a ripple and the tide. My friends, this Earth day, there is a tidal wave of anguish, of pain, of fear and of anger. If those of you who are truly workers of Light, of the Divine, representing the God-self, send those ripples in the effect of truth, send those ripples in the effect of joy, of love so that an avalanche of truth will hit the planet neutralizing the hatred and doubt and sorrow. For this Earth plane will have to go into balance before you move another step.

So I'd like you to think about that just for a moment. In simplicity is where truth always is. When you hear the intellect in those who speak of deeper intellectual thoughts, know that it is not always the highest and the best. The truth is simple. It always has been and it always will be. Truth is a very short word. It has five letters. You have five fingers. You have five human senses. And in your truth you use every sense that you have excluding one and that exclusion you must include. It is your common sense. Common sense is a God-given gift. There are five sides to a star as you draw it on the Earth. The fifth chakra is the chakra of communication. When you utilize truth and speak your truth, use your voice. Always thinking and speaking as if God is sitting next to you and as if an angel has just moved into the room. And if you live your life in that accordance, knowing that ever-loving Divine presence is truly always in your field of being, you will never be outside of your truth. I ask Michael to come back this evening.

Michael:

You know, I need to answer something so that you don't get any silly thoughts about things. In the first place there is no time in spirituality. So there really is not a schedule similar to a workman's schedule that you have on the Earth plane.

I've been hearing some chatter that I am in charge for two hundred years. I am not in charge of anything. God is in charge of all things and as a servant of Divine Beingness, working as an Archangel, I just am! None of the Archangels have ever made claims to being in charge for any particular period of time. We all represent a different aspect of God. Someone else mentioned that I was an alien. I am not an alien. I may be alien to the Earth. I may be alien to some people who do not communicate with Angels, but I am not an alien per se as your human definition.

To continue with the teaching I want to say that one of the real important parts of spiritual work, as I have said before, is humor. You have to understand that humor is the sound of the bells of the Angels as it transcends through the Universe. Humor is what breaks up energy. That is why I say laugh. When you laugh you create healing. You break the stagnation. That is why people at funerals have that nervous laughter. If you can really get someone who is in a lot of pain to laugh then you are doing so much healing. It is one thing to feel love in that seriousness and serenity but it is another thing to be turned around and energized by humor. You need to laugh. If you are going to do any ceremonial work, you have to laugh.

You have to laugh! There has to be something inside of each and everyone of you that you promise yourself that during the course of the day you are not going to just smile. That is not good enough. That means you are almost there. You are going to laugh. The thing is that you really need to be humorous. During the heaviness of this Earth change, during the heaviness of this time of transition, during this heaviness of the time when so many people are connecting with God, their Angels, their Masters and their teachers, during this time when so many people are opening and becoming aware of God there is such a serious air that people are forgetting to laugh.

The most spiritual person in the world is not the one with the deep furrow in the brow, the one who speaks like a funeral dirge going up the street. I mean, let's face it. That's what some people think that spirituality is. They think that you must be serious. That you must wear black. Dim the lights. Burn some incense. Light a candle. No it's about being light and humorous. There's enough pain and suffering on the Earth. Be light. Be humorous. Laugh.

What we're going to do is end. Through Divine Love, Divine Light and Divine Wisdom I give thanks for Sananda and the Master teacher. I give thanks for the Christ presence and I give thanks and so it is.

Your Thoughts Become Your Reality
Michael: July 28, 1994

We give thanks this evening and we ask that the healers, teachers and the masters encased in the beauty and the guidance of God's divine power come into the room so that the beings gathered here this evening are able to hear the words brought in from the Highest of the High to those in the physical plane.

We would like to start by saying that what you may think of yourself is your prayer.

Human beings in the physical form (we're not talking about human beings in the dream state or human beings who have transcended their human bodies.) We're talking about human beings in the physical form because the drug of illusion, the way you see the world, is so thick, the fog is so heavy that when you do have personal, emotional and physical problems and you start keeping your focus in these areas, as you start looking at these areas, as you stay confined within that thought process, you build up steam and energy. The momentum and power behind the thought moves at such a rapid rate that it comes back into this realm of illusion. Many times you will see your condition manifest or you will see your disease process manifest before you can understand what it is that you have done to yourselves.

To make that a little bit clearer your thoughts are like the speed of light. It is very difficult to perceive how fast the speed of light is since it is just a theory and a concept for most of you sitting in the room. But to use a really simple example; when the sun has set, you are seeing the sun setting after it has set. That is how wonderful this world of illusion is. You never really get to see a real sunrise or sunset. You get to see it after it happens because light takes time to travel. Thunder takes time to follow after the vacuum of the lightening which is really going from the Earth up into the sky. It just looks like it's coming from the sky to the Earth.

What I am trying to say to you is that your thoughts, because they travel faster than the speed of light create a vacuum and depending on where your energy is determines what gets filled up in that vacuum. It could be the goop from the illusion, the stuff in the Universal mind and the stuff from the mind of group consciousness. Or when you pray your thoughts could be bringing in universal consciousness to fill in that void which then energizes your physiological being. And then your life feels good. That is the truth!

But! When your thoughts are zooming out into the Universe at the speed of light and you are focused in on the mundane, what comes in to fill that vacuum? What comes in to fill the vacuum is the stuff of the thoughts of the people around you. It is the energy field of group mind. So it is no wonder that when you are focused constantly in on worry that you are capturing the energy from the group mind that focuses in on worry. And the intensity of that energy comes in like a thunder clap reverberating throughout your being. Then the next thing you know as you look at your life, your life is either a blessed event or it is, as they say in England, a bloody mess.

Now we don't know how much more simple we can make this. It seems to us that no matter how simple we make it, you make it darn complicated because that is the beauty of human beingness. We get to hear you say that we make it sound so simple but it is so hard to do. You keep up that mantra, you keep up that affirmation and so it will be.

155

The truth is simple because life is truly simple when you really live the life in accordance to Divine Beingness.

Now there are variables for each and every individual that creates his or her own personal challenge. Some people are born with physical handicaps. So what does that do? Well, it makes their life more challenging in the physical sense to get things done in the physical plane. Some people are born with emotional handicaps. So what does that mean? In the emotional realm of things it is harder for them to get their emotions together. And some people are born with mental handicaps. So what does that mean? That means in the sphere in the realm of the mind they have challenges to overcome. And some individuals are having such a physic thunderstorm within their brain that it is almost impossible for them as individuals to focus in on the world around them because they are caught up in the physic storm within.

In this age that you call the twentieth century, you have a new science, a one hundred year old science, known as psychology. Human beings are coming together acknowledging each journey saying, "Yes, my journey is correct and my journey is correct and together we will develop a psychological theory." Now what we, in spirit, see being devoid, or de-void in their whole philosophy is the placement of God and Spirituality. In order to study pure intellect and human behavior as a science, you must incorporate God. Otherwise it is not a science at all. They say that they are studying the conscience. But, there is only God subconsciousness. They say they are studying the blue print in which a human being came in. They have forgotten about the past lifetimes, the karmic wheel that an individual has created for his or her self. Now we are not underestimating or undermining the science, for humankind does the best that it can do. But until the true science of metaphysics is brought into the sciences, those individuals who are emotionally, physically and mentally handicapped or challenged, will remain so because they are receiving an archaic form of treatment. A treatment of putting a Band-Aid over a gaping wound, so to speak. For the true healing process comes about when you combine the science of the mind with the science of the Divine. The Divine is the only science.

You must never forget that your challenges are your own! No one has done anything to you. This is a repeat. No one can do anything to you unless you personally allow them to take the keys and the ownership papers away from you, which is your title to your personality self. What we hear on the spiritual plane from more individuals is: "How could they do this to me?" Why do you sit there? Why do you allow it to happen? Where is your free will? Where is your capability to side-step a situation and say, "I am a Divine, regal child of God. How dare you treat royalty so shamefully and how dare you dishonor the royalty that lives within your bloodline?"

What we are going to do is end. Through Divine Light, Divine Love and Divine Wisdom we give thanks and so it is.

About the Author

Denise R. Cooney has been a teacher and student of metaphysics for over twenty five years. Her other books include:

Beyond a Master
What on Earth Is Happening

Denise can be reached for information on classes or readings by writing to her at:

P.O. Box 196
Franklin Lakes, New Jersey 07414
U.S.A.

Denise recommends reading books written by Catherine Pondes, Meher Baba, Sister Thedra, Nick Bamforth and any books from the Unity Church.